WA

WAY OUT THERE

Lyrical Essays
Michael Daley
Aequitas, New York

FIRST PRINTING

AN AEQUITAS BOOK
AEQUITAS IS AN IMIPRINT
OF PLEASURE BOAT STUDIO: *A Literary Press*
201 W. 89th Street
New York, NY 10024
Tel/Fax: 888-810-5308
email: pleasboat@nyc.rr.com
URL: www.pleasureboatstudio.com

COVER PHOTOGRAPH: *Desolation Angels* by Steven R. Johnson
BOOK DESIGN: OLD DOG NEW TRICK

ACKNOWLEDGMENTS
    I wish to express my thanks to the editors of publications
where versions and sections of these essays and some of the
poems were first published: *Clinton Street Quarterly, Common Ties,
Dalmo'ma, Duckabush Journal, Electrum, Homeless Not Helpless, In
Our Hearts & Minds, Margins, Original Sin, Poets 1984, Prairie
Schooner, Raven Chronicles, Refugees: an Anthology, RosehipPlum
Cherry, Seattle Review, The Temple, Working the Woods Working the Sea*
    Additionally, I owe a debt of gratitude to Jack Estes for
his continued belief in this book, to Jennifer Moyer for her sharp
eye, to Bill Bridges for *his* eye not to mention insight, to the
ghost of Laddie, to Finn and Steve for the kick in the butt that
photo gave me, to Tim for reality checks, to Theo for tolerating
snapshots of his youth, and to Kathy who edited the oldest and
lived through the latest of these essays with love and grace.

In memory of my father, Francis Martin Daley, and
for Rebecca Faye Louzan

It is certainly a great folly, and one that is almost always punished, to go back to the places of one's youth, to want to relive at forty the things one loved or greatly enjoyed at twenty.
—Albert Camus, *Lyrical and Critical Essays*

TABLE OF CONTENTS

For the One Among Us Who Will Be the First to Die...11

I
When I Return...23
At Any Moment...41
Passengers...49

II
My First Poem...59
How I Changed...73
Love & Hate...75
"All Watched Over by Machines of Loving Grace"...77
A Letter to Dan Peters...91

III
Hibakusha...101
Witness...104
Silver Sea...113
The Land, the Boycott & the Unarmed Muse...118
The Duckabush, the Dosey & the Hamma Hamma...120
Climate & Currency...125
Running on Empty...141

IV
Of Aphrodite's Deathless Smile...157
Hungarian Notebook...171
Wild Art ...197

FOR THE ONE AMONG US WHO WILL BE THE FIRST TO DIE

New England's flaming trees seem preternaturally lit by mid-October. They glow that way only a short time. Boys in my school barely noticed, stopped rarely to save the leaf running with poppy and apple colors. Ice formed every night for a week. One of the brothers walked out on the pond each morning and held a ruler to the weakest edge. In my second year of high school, when I was the youngest of thirty-five seminarians, I learned to skate.

The ice he approved glistened until the fifteen-minute break between classes. In ties, dirty jackets, pocked skin, and too-short pants, we skidded on shoes that scuffed the smooth plate. It was nine inches thick. I was fascinated by the clarity of the Miles River running below, branches submerged beneath my feet, leaves in the current fluttering hopelessly away from the chasm under the bridge. Deep, the eyes of fish bulged up at me.

For those fifteen minutes everyone was kind, laughing or yelling over echoes clipped by metal trees. Some had sticks and pucks and dared one another to a quick game. Chasing someone to the far end, near the bridge where the current was strong beneath the ice, I saw the Miles twist through tufts and hassocks frozen onto our flooded pond, a primal seeping under pitched voices. Then a boom over the ice, the whole solid piece rang, a nine-inch deep seam snapped across the pond, hair-thin fissures shooting from its sides. Charged with adrenalin, we ran, slipped, and leapt to the frozen banks.

All fall I struggled to learn to skate. "*Arma Virumque cano Troiae,*" I recited, lugging the skates to the ice. "*Qualis apes . . .*

,"grunting, tightening the lacings. *"Quo usque tandem abutere, Catalina, patientia nostra?"* as I fell. And fell again. And finally after much care, began to slide slowly across the ice and forgot to brace for the fall, lifting one foot then the other to push off and skate.

During Christmas vacation my uncle brought his niece from the other side of the family to our house. The adults left us alone on a pond and we skated all afternoon. For a student celibate, an afternoon with a girl, even a cousin, was dangerous. I didn't dwell on the danger, but spent the day with a coiled tingle behind the navel. After skating we talked in the living room and I inhaled a particular scent for the first time. Her body gave it off; I was amazed. Foul like sweat, musty and wool and some sweet drop I couldn't define or later rub from memory. She went on talking and she didn't smell how beautiful she was. Returning to the seminary after the holiday would have been more terrible had the pond not been frozen. For by this time my efforts were paying off. I was crazy about skating and I knew I might forget everything but that scent of hers if I skated hard on a cold wind.

An expedition of skaters was headed up the Miles. An all-day trek, grueling, freezing in the wind; we would expend our energies on the ice and by evening even those like me, who still fell often, would return as veteran skaters. The French Canadians were going. I was very impressed by them. They came to study with us and some of them had little English but more vitality than the rest of us, and an intensity which transformed them when they were at prayer into simpletons. Jean Lefevre, with his red hair and gapped teeth, looked foolish in chapel piety, his small head in his hands, rocking back and forth, such a sinner. I wondered what his confessions were like. But on the ice he couldn't wait, and skated with untied lacings dangling like wings from his ankles, assured and poised as always on ice, cajoling us slowpokes in his thick accent.

12

While our little band located onto the ice and waited 'til everyone was ready, I stood at the fringe of a hockey scrimmage. The players had shoveled enough snow off to drag goalie nets. The seniors were practicing with Father Brown, an excellent skater. Jim Forrest was in the goal and two other boys played defense against the priest. He swaggered onto the rink laughing at them 'til they took his challenge to play him one against three. He was a man of purpose, I noticed, and like many Canadians, scrupulously unpretentious. He skated around them with the puck, outmaneuvering like some odd ballerina, shin pads clattering in cold air, the echoing shish-shish of skates and hockey sticks clapping over the pond. He wheeled the puck in and out of the defenders, teasing them before challenging the goal. Jim was covered by shoulder pads, shin guards, huge gloves, and a face mask. He eased out and placed himself squarely in front of the goal; though bundled, he looked too fragile. When the priest skated very fast toward him, Jim swiped the ice, but missed the puck. Father Brown prepared to deliver it into the goal when Forrest lurched to the right and set himself as an obstacle, which made the priest laugh before ramming him full force onto the ice. Then it was over and he slid the puck in the empty goal. I was impressed. Jim didn't move for three minutes. I had never thought a priest capable of that, and I installed Father Brown in my chamber of idols.

While some made sure Jim got up, the leaders of the skating party headed off. There had been snow and wind the night before, so we had to pick our way through rough ice. To leave the pond, we walked on skates up a trail to a small brick bridge where the road, punctuated by spiny birch, crossed the Miles River. I lagged behind to hobble up and crawl over the bridge without anyone looking. I crammed gravel into my knees and palms, and slid down the embankment to the other side. But as I stepped onto the ice, someone shot out from under the bridge. Lefevre had come behind me and hurled himself at top speed flat onto the ice and slid beneath the three-foot clearance.

Instantly he jumped up, grinned at me, and ran on his skates to catch the group. I watched him weave in and out of mounds frozen to the body of the river. He tilted and veered between mound and weed patch. Icy wind had caught eddies the night before and kept them in a lumpy fabric. I watched him leap and kick one skate up like a rudder, and lean his bare head into wind that clattered frozen cattails against one another. Way past his head, the dark forms of the others teetered like masts in a small regatta on twists of the flat river.

Now I was alone. There was wind and the soft brush of dead weed. The scrape of my skates. I went leisurely and slowly, studying how the shape of my shadow lengthened and shortened as a man whose arms and feet could bend deliberately and evenly, fluid with care. A man of purpose. I brooded over the image. As a priest that's what I would be, yet the image was appalling. A week ago a girl was skating beside me, laughing in a unique way. Marie, my cousin. At the beginning she'd said something I've heard only once or twice since, in bars or at parties. We were skating near small clusters of people on the bank, near a building. Someone fell on the ice and they joked to make him feel better. He was tall and wore a flamboyant scarf. His accent from the Deep South would have been enough of an anomaly, but his skates were unusual too—black figure skates, the kind hardly anyone wore; no one at school anyway had anything but hockey skates, stout and scuffed. "What time of year is it?" they asked. He was holding the back of his head. He looked up at the sky and with a grimace said "Yule," at which they all laughed. My cousin took my arm and led me back to skating. She said very seriously, "Tell me a lie." I looked at her, but her face was turned down at the ice. Then with a grin to cover what I might have taken as precociousness, she was a girl again: "I'm Al Capone's granddaughter." We both laughed.

14

As much as I was a beginner with her, so was I in the spiritual life as well. My rites of puberty were superimposed on the Spiritual Exercises. As a way of purging our souls after the vacation, we immediately held the monthly Exercise for a Happy Death. It was during my Examination of Conscience before confession that images of her came back strongest. The laughter, her smiles and jokes, remembering we actually held hands a few minutes—all this was most secret. I scoured my conscience for the bit that made sin, but kept losing the thread, and stopped searching, and knelt there in chapel, remembering.

During the two days of the Exercise for a Happy Death I was permitted to speak with Father Cardillo. Although I had entered school only a few months earlier, he was already familiar with my abysmal moodiness. His office was a small cubicle near the main lobby; the frosted pane on the door held an etched image of the Sacred Heart, and you could look through either the heart itself or the thorns and dagger to see who was spilling his soul, who was crying, who was to be sent home. No one had given me so much attention when teenage depression haunted me. "What's wrong?" I fidgeted in the leather seat across from his desk. The face I made could have indicated I was less than comfortable; he continued to read his mail and question my soul. "I think I'm going crazy or something." For months he'd been completing his psychology doctorate at Boston College. Tapping a silver letter-opener against pale fingernails, he leaned back into the swivel chair. The squeaking and the short rolling sounds of the wheels signaled everything was all right now, we could talk. "Do you know who the President is?" His eyes went up in a funny way toward the ceiling. "Johnson." "What year is this?" "What?" "Do you know when your birthday is?" He wasn't letting me be crazy today. My cousin Marie . . . how strange I felt. I didn't commit a sin, and I couldn't stop remembering her. Why did I feel guilty?

It may have been his silences I learned from, if I learned anything. Seven years later I knocked on his door to say I had

15

decided in the middle of the night, the last moment before renewing the vows, to leave the Order because I could not be celibate. In all those years his gestures indicated when he thought I was right or wrong. He was generous about Marie; there'd been a cousin in his early days too. "She would have had me," he said, "but her mother came along just in time." I tried to imagine the state of panic I would have felt. He didn't elaborate details, yet I could picture his young, buck-toothed face wrinkled in distress, the cousin unfastening his clerical collar, an image I'm sure he didn't mean me to take. "Look, try to understand what you're attracted to. Isn't it her body because its form is different from yours and everyone you know?" That sounded right. "Well? Is it breasts? Sure, breasts are lovely. We enjoy them. We'd love to touch them, they attract us. Do you know what breasts are for?" It was several seconds before I realized he wanted an answer I presumed I couldn't give. Chagrined, I said they were for the baby. "The baby, that's right. I don't have babies myself, only the baby at Christmas, and every morning when I say Mass. Do you want that? Now, why do you think a girl's hips are wider than a boy's?" But this was disappointing; he must have seen that. We can say Mass and breasts become breasts, hips hips. A bag of flesh. That is why we control our eyes, our ears, every thought. "The problem you're having is of course common. You may always have it. Thoughts are hard to cleanse. Okay, this is the Exercise for a Happy Death. Imagine if you will that every thought for the next few days might be your last. That's hard, isn't it? I know it is, but try. What would you want it to be, your last thought? The girl you skated with?"

By now I was all but walking around tufts of grass. I'd already caught a blade under the skate and fell. My knees were sore and wet and I was cold. I tried to concentrate: to become a man of purpose, I must get down the Miles and come back a skater. The river lay before me like a desert and the wind, though slight,

16

flapped in my ears and froze the hairs of my nostrils. He could have gone harder on me. In private he did not come off as severe as he did in public. The logic of his talk two nights before had run counter to my question, "Why am I tempted like this, if called to be a priest?" My cousin Marie, everything about whom was wonderful and alien, could lure me from my vocation. Yet, he explained, if I have a vocation the Blessed Mother will protect me. If I have a vocation and leave, I have broken a promise to her, and should I die, I might drop directly into hell.

As my skates cut awkwardly the rough surface of the river, I felt sure I had a vocation. Reluctant to dismiss thoughts about Marie, I fell to wondering about my last thought before death, taking it as seriously as I could, bundled as I was against a cold that couldn't fail to make me feel alive. The penultimate prayer before the close of the Exercise frightened me most, despite another sermon when Father Cardillo tried to witness his funeral. The prayer leader intones the title and the entire body of male voices, some deep, others croaking or high-pitched, rolls off the list of last particulars of the body's decay. The leader says, as if hoisting a beer stein, "For the One among Us Who Will Be the First to Die." "Lord have mercy, Christ have mercy." Everybody chants to a hypnotic beat in night chapel like Bushmen who might utter poetry to wonder if they will always be, except "one among us" could include the fallen and burning trees. As I moved over ice, this prayer coursed through my efforts to evade the memory of Marie, but as for my last thought, I couldn't envision it. My nose was dripping and the little bit I gained on the skating party vanished when I calculated how far they were. Was that it then? A trance we were in? Did we know nothing, or did we learn to know nothing? Did we pray out of primitive fear or did we understand our lives? Did we run toward the Light or from it? As much as I loved that priest, trusted and craved his counsel, I never told him about the brother who tried to rape me the year before I skated the Miles. Back in Boston I'd felt privileged to get to play table tennis after school. I realized what

17

was happening only after he chased me around the table, caught me, and began to pull down my pants, tugging me onto his lap where the folds of his black cassock hid an erection. I was dizzy, straining my sense of reality against disbelief. This was a person I liked and trusted. Flying down the steps while zipping up, I wondered what my mother was saying to my father at that moment.

 I disguised the event: it didn't happen. Yet for twenty years I have had a recurring dream. In a damp catacomb, lit by weak lamps, a banner hangs above the door: "Those who cannot fend for themselves must be placed on an altar." I am standing beside the altar, having carried a beautiful woman. Half the room is too dark to see. She is blond, and in a black gown with bare shoulders. I found her earlier that day in daylight, like a scene from *La DolceVita*, but in the most Marilyn Monroe style possible. We've made love somewhere on a wooden bench; she wanted to leave the park almost fainting with heat and the fear of oppressive eyes . I told her I'd take care of her and she sank into my arms like a trusting child. The room is an alcove, a sanctuary. I am standing guard by her head. Doors open at the dark end of the room and two disfigured people enter. "What do you have to say about this?" says the one in the lead. When he gets close enough, I see it is Father Cardillo. The man behind him is the brother pederast. They have misshapen heads. The priest's is worse, a crater dent on the right side of his overly large forehead. His hair has thinned and his eyes, always big, are magnified by the hollow around them. Blue veins on his face are the shape of a horrible insect. He is in the same black cassock, which sweeps dirt like some deformed artisan's apron. The brother is his disciple. They rush toward me, toward the altar. I try and fail to scream, ready to fight. They are so ugly and menacing they are ghouls. I have been expecting them; I must ask a question about love and how will I be able to express it now, but my rage is so great they flee by a door in the sacred wall which turns to light as they pass there.

*

I heard the scraping of skates behind me and turned, surprised that someone was rushing up. Hugein in his woolen coat, a scarf about his nose and wearing sunglasses, George Stanton, a junior I didn't know well, skated awkwardly toward me, about to shatter my privacy. I was relieved I wouldn't have to think, but in a panic because we were going to speak, or else he might push me out of the way. His irregular strides scuffed the ice; his arms lurched out from his sides; he was getting closer and there was no room to pass. When he was almost on top of me, he turned abruptly, annoyed to find me standing there, and skated through a thin mound toward a patch of open ice… where he plunged to his waist in the river. He looked ridiculous, sunglasses floating beside him, arms waving in all directions, angry at himself. His forehead creased, he looked into the chipped ice floating onto his coat and spread his hands out. He was standing on something. Then he leaned onto an ice block, it broke, and he fell forward. I didn't know what to do. He was the older boy; I hoped he would tell me. But he kept bobbing around in the water, flapping his arms higher above the ice each time. He was yelling words I couldn't understand, as if at himself. He appeared to want me not even to look at him. I lay on the ice, and my wool pants soaked through instantly. Holding the nearest clump of weed, I stretched my legs toward him. "Grab my skates! Grab my skates!" I yelled loud as I could over his splashing and cursing. But he lunged forward, as if he could get out of it by himself. The ice snapped again. I twisted around to get closer, mad now because he ignored me. "Grab the skate, Stanton! Stanton!" He paid attention at the sound of his name. "Grab the skate!" Finally he did, and his weight pulled on my ankles. I was afraid I wouldn't hold to the clump of weeds. "Pull yourself," I called again and again, and I pulled too, getting my hand a little farther into the weeds. I started crawling more or less, over the ice. When I looked back at him, he was straining, yet his eyes were incredibly alert.

19

"Pull your . . . self . . . pull! Pull!" I could feel him tugging all through my legs. He was very heavy. My clothes were frozen, my pants stuck . Finally, when his body was on thick ice, he jumped from the water as if propelled. I lay there, panting and sweating for just a second before I made Stanton flap his arms, then slapped at his legs and feet, yelling at him. He stared toward school at the hard ice as I slapped him and kept telling him how stupid he was until I got tired. When I stood in front of him to look for signs of shock, he was glaring at me. Then he turned and began awkwardly again, slowly, to skate in the direction of school. If he was embarrassed, I didn't know why. He appeared so dignified to me as I watched him make his way on iced weeds; he never looked back, lumbering from side to side as if hypnotized. Later we would become friends, two boys alienated from their schoolmates' more direct expressions of feeling and who much later would shy away from those raw moments of outrage and love that friends and colleagues would succumb to in the face of global cruelty and arrogance. Over the wide river covered with snow, he was the only moving thing, dwindling into a small iced object on the horizon. He was almost at the bridge when I turned to look toward the farthest bend of ice at snow and wild meaningless weeds. I couldn't go in either direction. I could barely see the others upriver, a world incapable of change. I was at the center of a large floating avenue of deaths. Figures in the distance wore bright colors. Although they were going nowhere, they were dressed to dance.

I

It *seems a desperate time of the year.*
Apples, the last, should have been picked
but for the unseasonable cold, unnatural frost.
   It comes after so long a penitent waiting,
through the cold, red cold apple
the fingers touch. And just, you hope,
the one person's
         from tree to you.
But what happens there in the orchard
takes many hands, many baskets to bushel
to grocer, to home.
      Theirs are the first fingers—
having carried their bodies with so much care
across our borders—
         to lift the apple from the branch.

Opposite Paradise, Lost Eden, it is the one
who first slunk across the border,
so unlike that Adam who named, and ate,
and then knew evil,
      and fled the quintessential anger—
The Angerer,
   even while we carve the bright bloody groove
of autonomy and distance
                  into the human heart.
It is the one who entered the garden fleeing
the great wilderness of raw wounds
            who picks our fruit.

WHEN I RETURN

Our Lady of the Broom

When the Border Guard in his little booth told me just out of earshot of anyone but his partner that I was entering a foreign country, it was in a sardonic and menacing tone no one had ever used on me before; I didn't know if twenty dollars U.S. would stand in for my missing passport. Two weeks earlier I had interviewed five young men living on the streets of a major American city. All fled separately from the war in their country. Combining a cheap vacation with more research on the plight of refugees, I left San Diego that morning to return three weeks later to the same McDonald's, a place where one of our first public shootings, now frequent news items, had just occurred; more people wrapped in blankets sat in corners, and my traveling companion of several years had begun to sound like the man in the booth.

Why had I come there that morning? To watch a woman sweep her useless porch? The light of the world was free in the field where no one smiled but into the arms of cactus. A boy leapt a cyclone fence. Embrace me, thin donkey, you two roosters! Loose bits of thatch lay out under a star, sticks for walls leaned on a breeze. The water hadn't poisoned me; wells were clear. Beside the driver's Virgin, Jesus dangled from the mirror. We pass a buzzard shadow and raise the dust. Pictured in my magazine, a man squats beside the trees, a little girl squinting beside him; he is her father, or uncle, a brother who held her when they ran silent in the jungle setting their faces for the grand world, pretty as it turns, facing in opposite directions.

Too hot on the street, we walk to the plaza —"The Saint of America" scrawled under the dark Xerox of the murdered Archbishop. Twenty years ago I too took the vows—in the seminary's little chapel, but I was on crutches. I pictured myself getting up from the pews where we novices listened to one another promise chastity, obedience, and poverty. I was afraid to dramatically hobble away from so solemn a ceremony, everyone knowing I'd given into those doubts which had pursued the years I'd prepared for this moment. The martyr makes me tremble, or the spell I was under has charged the air around the church, and I almost faint. A small man named Ishmael asks the time. I try to tell him in my brutal Spanish. He studied marine biology, and wants to spend the night in our hotel; we have the extra bed, after all. I'm half-awake through the night, my wallet a lump beside my ear, as he reads the book of poems I carry in my pack, Roque Dalton's. In the morning he grins— "Poems of revolt," he says, the kind he likes. Every street a battle or a hero's name, we step out on The Fifth of May. "Take good care of my friend," he says and winks at both of us, an inside joke, and enters the crowd to go sell tacos from a cart. Most nights he sleeps on the beach, our escaped marine biologist. The moon from a crystal tumbler poured a flood tide over the street last night; he may have told himself when he spotted me in my sunglasses, the sea will not be my bed tonight. Why have I come here this morning? The air cleans my lungs and I nod on and on to the boy pilot who takes coffee with us to practice *ingles* on our map to the Sea of Cortes.

Two girls in an orange orchard watch our bus and pull their skirts, the mountain range behind them breaking sunset on its spine. Across the aisle Roque points them out. He has a generous face, but effeminate. He was born in a southern town; he crosses the border Tuesdays and takes the bus to work on Wednesday and Thursday. Brando's face, hair dyed blond. "What is your job?" I guessed he would say, "Waiter." Both of us too shy to mention the scar thick as my thumb on his skull, the tiny fight

24

promoter turns from the seat in front and smiles in the sweetest way. "The crowd last night yelled 'Kill, Roque! Kill! Kill!'" Grinding his little fists, his eyes linger over the champion, his smile pale as mountains pass us out the windows. Rocky invites us to a match, recommends a hotel, and humbly shakes our hands when they rise to leave. At their stop a baby near the door bites and kisses his young mother, butterflies in her hair.

Pressing into the crowd are two North Americans who hate the people. They can't stop complaining, even while some cows run from the bus with three goats. They speak badly about giving up their money, no matter it is so little; tired office workers from Duluth shopping for clothes on beaches where the real-estate people swim. Why have I come here this evening? To see a pregnant bride bow her head at the shrunken tip of California where we arrive for dinner on the bus they call "Three Stars of Gold?" Out the window are a girl her mother hasn't seen in weeks to run a brush or fingers through her hair, a young man grinning from a plastic hovel, and a horse with gold braid in its saddle. My love has been replaced by this shade that traveled far south to guide my Purgatory and leave. A man in Texas begged her to marry him. "I should have done it," she tells me, hills sorting a fan of light. "You and I will never marry. He kept talking about Jesus, peace, love, the baby brother he persuaded not to enlist and whom they set on fire. Three months living like a mouse, he walked to the border at the Rio Grande in checkered pants. How glad he was to be alive. Why?"

We were crossing the Sea of Cortes all night. An hour after the ferry landed in the morning, the two dark flags that are Joaquin's eyes were wavering over the highway heading east. It meant nothing to have run away, he told us. He cuts his coffee with Coca-Cola and drives four days and nights. White chapel bells ring the weddings on the bumpy coast of Vera Cruz, a banana cross on the map where his children are waiting, where at ball games and bus stops, and all cafés and beaches, where with bracelets and rings women remember him, and wait for

him. Four days of the white highway, cactuses and sand—
"Vallarta, Guadalajara, Jalisco," he says as he points out his
route—"Guanajuato, Hidalgo, Puebla." He drives a forty-meter
trailer to Vera Cruz. "What is your job?" "Frescas!" Cold drinks
he moves around the country.

  A newborn timid girl whose eyes meet ours knows
we're from another planet. Our skin is milk, and she cries for
hers rocking in the morning light on deck. At home—which
state was it? —a girl with a star cut by her eye yanked her baby
through a mall, and slapped him when he screamed. I'm sorry
to think of them now. This little girl almost singing begins to cry
and no one stops her. We were standing on deck with Joaquin,
she and I; since we couldn't leave the ship side by side, the
"tyranny of the couple" prevented our running away. "Do people
flee from other countries to come here and feel safe?" "We fly,"
Joaquin said. "We are all flying," waving at the driven breakers,
"me, you," his eyes fall back to the waves. He has asked me to
hire him; he knows the word "chauffeur," and supposes I'm
wealthier than I am, that I have more resources than three
hundred dollars in my wallet. I don't tell him that when I get
home I'll have to find a way to pay the rent. Even if I could hire
him, I wouldn't. I'm too preoccupied. This is that moment when
I recognize why I came here, why I fled to the needle of
California—so she and I could end a kind of scream, and float
off, dwindling alone in the "soul's boat" far beyond this cape of
land.

  Out on deck a hand I couldn't touch came from the
lump within its colored cloth. A baby as well as the breast was
covered in grass stains and soil from hills where daylight finds
no one's laundry, though jets swept the leaf with fire. While
they bombed in those hills, we two, despising one another,
crossed that sea, our eyes fixed on the wild breakers flashing in
moonlight. In gentle Joaquin's eyes, even Cortes might have
wept. As they bombed, we walked the deck; we didn't know,
while we watched the moon slide like a coin through the fog. In

a churchyard in my country uniformed teenage boys used to bark drills at a small infantry of third graders who were always giggling or poking one another. The cadet in new fatigues was leaning against a wire fence when a man in an oily uniform slouched past. He had just stirred something into a pot of stew and, cardboard duct-taped to his feet, hobbled off to find some salt. He stopped to watch. "I put my face in the Perfume River, and I drowned," he was smiling at me, "for this," his fingers lacing the chain-link fence.

While southern buses pressed against the station open to evening light, I remembered a dream in their language. All of us in white clothing, someone had disappeared from the foul bus shade, and dust had flowered into knots where the one we thought we knew had stood—an overturned green bus in wide leaf, sting sounds of cicada—acid drops of the sun steam and creak the rusty split rim of its left-front, whirring, clairvoyant wheel. Waiting to leave, I notice the brown straw brim of a man older than earth, a face of marble, black eyes turned to outer space, walking past the taxis with two donkeys, their reins loose in the clubs of his hands. One of their slow, rippled hides is draped in a white man's thigh, a sunburnt leg, the wide ass and probably pinched balls in a warm blue swimsuit sitting unsteadily; astride the other, a woman in new whites, straw hat, a *Nikon* brushing her nipple, stiffens her back, and talks over the rattling voices of the square in an English accented by Mid-Atlantic cities: "I haven't been there in eight years. I was walking past that alley when I heard her. She was pushed. I mean the guy put his hand right here and I was standing in the street I saw it on her chest Big Hands and veins standing out of the skin, the Glass stretching around her before it shattered her red dress bright as the middle of the day in the window I see the pattern of the dress right now Red in slow motion and with little white white little hearts Birds then the glass in splinters it was like music and she fell she bent her head up and she just crumpled there I said Harry I got to go

27

okay? And I go up 12th and next day take a ferry to Alaska I trembled three days."

Their voices remind me of my friend Bill who met a man living on the steps of the Public Library, spare-changing at the parking meters. "He said he was from Mexico, but the accent was wrong. 'No, you're not, You're from...'" and Bill named the man's birthplace. "My ear has improved," Bill told me. The library's shadow crept onto the car. He got out of the country when ten of his friends were killed at the beach. "They just want to see the water. It was a hot day. Why did they have to see the water?"

When we finally set off, it is almost dusk our bus heaves into, and at each twist of the road the wide deep leaf gets wider. On each a rider climbs the nugget steps and gives the driver nearly worthless pesos. The driver, a disciple of Jesus, a lovely John of the visions, has a Jesus on the dash, a Jesus inside a light bulb with thorns around his face; and jiggling from the mirror are Christmas booties, and pasted onto the mirror is the smallest Cross and Lamb I've ever seen. In the oak we pass, he points out Jesus. In the banana, and in the rainbow where the light is failing, a white bird—a dove—no, a gull is cracking over the waves and the tourists. In Sanctu Espiritu Hagios Haythoos, the baby and Mary are wearing napkins on their heads, he says, and that's Joseph in the straw hat. They are pilgrims in the gully. Jesus is their white dog, or else he is that boy in the baseball cap; he could even be this steer up ahead crossing the road, the baby in the front seat with a bull's gray eyes. He signs the 'V' and beeps to another bus, the only one we've seen on this road. Jesus is hot, I notice, crying from inside the light bulb. Jesus is the orange sun, the piss smell in *los bagnos* where Jesus sees me, takes my sin, and where he weeps. There in that grotto, our driver points, overgrown in thorn is a cross neon pink where Jesus without arms is surrounded by plastic flowers. Jesus is money, he says, "today and tomorrow and tomorrow and tomorrow." A woman boards the bus with babies and a drunk. She's the girl who washes whites out on a rock by the stream. "Thou art Pedro of a million pebbles." "Gracias," she says, "De Nada," and when she steps off a mile later, the graces of the earth rise to her feet from the narrow road in no town where there's no house, no wheel, and her two boys. But Jesus drives away too fast, laughing at the sound of breaking glass.

An old man from the river—so old he remembers Jesus. His grandsons, his daughter in his lap, his baby wife, hear the story—his horse. "Grandfather, where is Hey Zeus?" "Maria and Jose were very hot in Egypt fleeing the massacre of a colonel who was jealous enough to kill every baby. He couldn't find Jesus because three wise landowners paid a Coyote gold to take him to Egypt where it's hot, but they stayed until Jesus could talk. 'Mama,' he said, 'I'm ready for the temple bosses. I know language they can't speak. I have food they never tasted, my flesh they can't touch.' He was the blossom of roses where you get cut, a pilot singing over the palm leaf, a *campesino* that crawls in shadow." Smuggled into Sonora, the old man, whose hands are simply mended wounds, brown rope veins, tree-root fingers, gets off the bus in a dark little town. Why have I come here? To see this mad girl sitting down in the middle of the village street to feed her baby, who sucks and screams in ecstasy?

Jesus!

The cockroach, like lace on a bridal gown, races over the earth, and we do too to stop her staggering through dust and stars, though our skulls will all be piled in caves abandoned except for these quick brown shells, these wall-runners, drain-snipers, rust flakes in the shower, where to keep from killing three, I chase and shoo and apologize, and whinny when cold streams clog them in those grayish hairs the drain's teeth have left of what they've gnawed.

In the bay the fishing's going swell. Tomas poses with his pale blasé blue fin, six feet head to tail, before returning to a margarita at the pool. A slow and crowded marlin boat rounds the point, and motors near the rocks through the strong current of the gut. The captain makes his eyes like coin to buy silence for these men he's smuggling up the coast. A woman in a white petal dress leans to take a pebble from the beach. Her shoulders in the sun go quickly red, while the man who wants only to swim, waves from out there in the knee-high waves. The boat is full of skinny men who hide their eyes—also like money, and step from the dock; this one's house has turned to ash, that one's wife has saved his breath inside her baby's beach ball. They kick the sand and laugh, but soon they will split up; their lives are the drops of sea where I spend my coin on a woman who leans across a metal table. I see down her breast, beneath the moon, a satellite silhouetted.

Still early in December, we could make it home for Christmas. In the seminary by now, the Feast of Immaculate Conception, the priests tossed beans in a small bowl, voting on us who crowded outside the door. We hoped to learn whose bed was stripped, whose car door slammed as parents took them home. The priests were cleaning house: white beans in, black beans out.

When we do go north, a week before Christmas on a track in New England, I'll board the northbound train and she will wave, sheepish bag lady across the depot. These goodbyes pare me down to shavings on the floor, black beans in a black bowl. She warned if she could find anyone else to love, she would. I wanted to imagine she could change her course, and sit beside me as always. Instead, a woman in a flowered skirt passed my seat swinging her backpack down the aisle. A skein of magenta thread climbed her hip and fell over my fingers, and I remembered a film of her in Northern California. The fast train played it on Connecticut: she rushes into a small store, her same amused, frightened face leery of more pain, avoiding nothing, turns to smile at the camera. Her face was reeling through my fingers as the train cleared the track. On Immaculate Conception, feast of the impossible, a woman fucked an angel. Because by Christmas the House was swept of all who were not called, we named that feast Our Lady of The Broom.

At Isidoro & Aurora's

The priest said he spoke to them about Christ, his love and his mercy. The Indians listened attentively and ignored Christ completely. They think Christ must have been an Indian. . . . They don't care what the priest says, they can't see the value of praying to Christ, the sweet powerless bastard couldn't keep himself from being nailed to the wall. They only worship the saints, who are store dummies they've dressed up in their idea of rich people's clothing, lace tablecloths and dried fruits on a string for necklaces.

—— Jay Cantor, *Death of Che Guevara*

Children run crazy on cobbles and dirt, women toss buckets of water on the street. It overnight becomes dust truck wheels crush. Headlights of taxis with Christmas vacationers slow for firecrackers popping their windshields. The rosary over, a stout priest in the steeple drops sweets from a bucket, a farmer with chickens. The Piñata's strawberry crepe teeters and tangles his rope. A boy scoops candy, steps barefoot on a firecracker which explodes, grabs a lit one, lobs it to the crowd pecking for sweets, and runs a scummy puddle of dish water. We've heard the gruesome stories of the worms

Isidoro and Aurora have ten children. A daughter's baby runs into the stone street to gather candies taxis squash. His

31

mother lifts him to Aurora's eyes, and though she smiles placing our *paella*, he cries as if, too smart to run off, he grieves for all feasts to come. Years ago Isidoro lived in Sacramento and spoke some English. In a tiny migrant shack a broken heater gassed his first wife and three children. His name was erased from those orchards. I do not ask if he was legally in California. He'll never return, not even for avocados.

"Whenever you're ready, we can go home," my true love, my once true love, said to me, "We won't know each other anymore, when we've passed the border." We will, however, know the country we'll be crossing into. Lovers get married to land as well as to weeds and spiders in the furrows. Christmas is an ornament tossed in the highway. Isidoro's treasured second family would be Aztec art to our friends, collectors, at the house where we'll be staying, where wind bangs the mortgaged snow. "Why not stay here *por Navidad*?" His eyes are playing with me. I have already told him I'm almost broke, but I can't tell if he means for us to stay in his house, or in this town where once, the plaque says, a homeless Captain shipped out for the Philippines in Spanish clippers for the Pearl of Orient. Two of his daughters serve at the café and I love to watch them move; if I spent these days beside them, and nights near them under blessings of the family, I could not (could I?) actually touch this one with graceful legs, or the other with eyes cast down? Or does Isidoro picture us—and already seems to take back his offer, if there really was one—grim outsiders, their threadbare "marriage" half-relinquished, so foreign his youngest daughter will offer favored tamales, little stick dolls, and wonder aloud why we can't go home.

My money will run out before Christmas, I say, and I even tell him I'm a poet, but he laughs because I can never get the gender right. Kids with candy roar below the steeple. I savaged the language to say I wanted to meet a "refugee," to write about that life—yet I don't think I want to travel where they're from. He wouldn't want to go there either. Not now.

32

Beheadings, impaling, rapes, disembowelments, and terror are loose there, as are sadness and torture. Perhaps, since I didn't go to Vietnam and don't know war, I can be told a pregnant woman was killed, and the father was decapitated before their children, and I can repeat this now, remaining calm. I can return to North America and watch the nightly news without wincing.

Isidoro's not enough. He was illegal in California, but now owns acres of coconut, a truck with his name on the door, and a world full of daughters. He didn't ask why I wanted to meet the refugee women. If anyone had asked, I'd have run off, caught haunting the slums. "Two women in the next town are very pretty waitresses." Tomorrow he sells coconuts from his field. He doesn't know if they'll talk, if I come. They're very pretty. He starts to say more, and then looks, as if afraid, around the square. The youngest daughter serves tacos and some kind of fish across the street. Twelve years old and with an alarming stare: she passes, hiking the back of her skirt around her waist, and tucks crisp orange bills, her tips, into her underpants, and skips across the street. A boy pees against a wall. Then some teenage girls walk past us. Isidoro blinking looks behind us till they're gone. "They . . . fuck . . . *si?* unnerstan'. . . *por denaro* . . They make good money . . . very pretty," rubbing a thumb on a fingertip. I had forgotten about this. I look across the street. I say I understand to the black puddle. I want to say in Spanish, "That's too bad," but nothing comes. *"Es mal,"* he says. "Yes."

They have a three-year-old girl, born to one of them here in this country. They have no husbands. The men are fishing farther north, but "few here, few yobs," he says. The fourth truck tonight from *Cooperativa de Pescadores* eases through the kids and firecrackers. The bar by our pension is loud beside the *Cooperativa*. Usually, when we pass, so white I think they'll jeer at us, or grab her arm or blond hair, I feel how far south we really are. The earth spins, my skin burns through to the wet cobblestone. *Norteamericano, turista, yanqui,* it's in their eyes. *Gringo.* They think we must be lost; for them there is no America. We step more

33

quickly; I count my money again and vow it will be different when I return. Plath said, "We could be Japanese," and we could, but like Japan, alpha project, only A-bomb-received-nation, we could wear a face famous for surviving our own execution. "No yobs, no yobs," Isidoro keeps repeating. I can come tomorrow. "When they go north, they left the women here." Licensed and checked often by the *medicos*, they raise the children of the dead. "The only work is what these women do, and they are very pretty."

      The country is wearing only her light, and the poor are laughing with gold in their teeth. The Indian who even when I learn the question cannot direct me. *Dirigame por favor?* "Senor," the man beside him tells me, "he has another language, Senor." This one has a young man's pool-hall smile, but they are both selling me the roasted chicken. Voices, also without language, whispered just as informatively one night in the Rockies on a train I rode through western towns—western towns! I love it so! To have come west looking for something and all there was was snow sweeping entire states. "In Yakima, when it's gettin' that time of year," an older white woman's subdued train voice mumbled, "they have armed battles with them illegal aliens come to pick the hops." And another, with a European accent two seats behind mine reading aloud: *"My soul wanted to be a flag and they want to transform it in the temple of merchants. In the gray histories of snow, there will be recorded a city in a desert."* Or later, across the crushed heart of Montana streaked by its own iced poor, where farms were empty shells, a starved man held his chest. His voice in a train crossed into the West, clutching a memory in his bone lap. When America stretches and stirs, fatigue and enterprise embrace and dance. From his house or the office, the architecture of a late 19th-century myth, a rumpled man fends off Love, solid as art in arches and gargoyles where he has written history and pressed his portrait, and moans with Richard, "Sent into this breathing world, dogs bark at me." But now, on simple still leaves, memories of other rain adjust to the sound. Coconuts scrape

34

under the tide, and the boys drag something another tide will remember. Venus, her hair shaken into the weedy palm, scatters through far-off lightning a bag of coins. The United States is a planet away, the neon and disco its rude tax on the orchestra of the dark.

Our corner room feels chilly as another pale bulb expires. Maps along one wall shiver in the fan breeze; volcanoes on the paper are restless on its pins. The shadows of the world appear to walk across the wall. We twist on our sunburns to try love one more time. Knowledge of solid objects disappears, and her face becomes a shell in my palms, parentheses to hold fog. I am the dress a bride carried to her chamber while rowers sang on a lake. She stammers and prays. In neon through the window, the blue witness limps and leaps away.

Out the window in the grotto, tiers of devotion candles flutter in a garden. Two women on chairs say a novena in shawls beside the Virgin who glows amid rosaries and gifts. The breeze stroking their skirts crosses our open window and bears incense. "Will you make love to Isidoro's women?" She asks, almost asleep, "Does his wife know he knows them? He won't tell her. They'll want to though; they'll think you're rich." A rooster explodes in our quarter. A hair of lightning breaks the east. Thunder shoots around us, rain sheds its ribbons, and I jump out of bed; a slave tossing in the ship's dark hold, I'm terrified of lightning. In moments it stops, and the old women's candles still miraculously burn. Our electric fan twists in half-circles. She holds me in the receding thunder till I sleep. "We are memorizing every muscle and bone of the thing we are dropping from a high place," a voice in my dream says, "I have bent my face to the Perfume River." Tattoos are on his wrist, the numbers ice blue. "I married her they would have sent back." In the doorway, she's afraid of him. She's still in the bed of her husband. "At first I didn't love her." My face is in the mirror, with a tattoo on my cheek. In an

35

olive jacket, her hair tied back, she sits with others in the open military truck. Every bone was crushed to powder. So much so fast.

After the rain has wedged into palm and a migrant moth wrinkled the puddle, the lights along the Gulf's bowl were tipped in burnt blue, leaves flapping upward. A mile north a rusty cock sang, and his wings ripped up the roof late for work, driving his hens to nibbling. On the rich coast the flare of dawn pierced a rooster's fan. A fat man was already fishing a lake when roses robed the trees, filled the bullet holes with shadow, and sprayed the feathers of the skinny singer who paraded in daylight, and graced the street, spluttered ripe and breakable notes while a man raving at his own wounds held poems up to fly wild. Farther north the rooster was busy and the light was harder. The sun bled onto his tail feathers, and his brood crowded the map. When the cocks ran from the light, their beaks stained in shit, an old man with ringworm eyes stepped from a door and said, "Are you my son?" His airless bones shuddered, surprised by feet on a highway. Dogs stirred in the sierra. At Acapulco near the airport a woman from Massachusetts cracked awake. A starving rooster has waited all night to uncage the morning. And in our village the one to guard us from dawn's ambush is Captain Emiliano, who brays at midnight, sings by noon, and coughs at any hour. On a leash, his lava wings hatch his vexations, blaze the comb, and menace our feet when we pass on our way to coffee, banana, and papaya. The women march with empty bags to buy the early fruit. Emiliano, a gangster rooster, lifts his arsenal again, his bright tail feather like a royal cape. The shadow races west, Zapata flies again—skinny chest, scrawny feathers, tall bird with a rag comb, talons wrapped in loose pebble.

In his café, Isidoro Trujillo is sun king, and we have *cervezas* early. He will not be going with coconuts to the whorehouse today. The women work at La Cantina Ra Sol in the next town. Has he thought better of bringing the gringo to hookers? Or has Aurora stirred him in the first stripes of dawn

36

to say he will not do this? To say their camp of sticks was napalmed when guerrillas might be there. To say a corpse was bobbing in the river. You run past crates of peach resembling famous ears, past flickering light, papaya, coconut, lime. Hallucinogenic birds breakfast on rain, a fragment of leaf tangled in your hair.

They knew your name at the Ra Sol, Rosario. The women have oval faces, teeth angled like gravestones. Their oiled arms shine, bringing beer. Men strut in the dust to practice the wound of love, and touch themselves in public while they stand behind a *gringa's* bold reflection in the shoe store window, and weave red combs across their hair. Both of those women quit Cantina Ra Sol, the waitress says, so slow even I can understand. They point me toward the beach. "Hotel La Playa, not far. La Playa! Rosario's there. She has a daughter." They giggle about why she quit Ra Sol, "a *Norte Americano*, Joe." As I read her my notes, I remembered how they smiled. "*Estar bien . . . con Usted . . . Usar . . . mi . . . grabadora?*" I held it toward her. This is my tape-recorder, *grabadora, maquina.* May I use it? "Si." She said so twice, but I was still unsure. "*Mi preguntas por favor.*" The only refugee I could have asked, because of Isidoro Trujillo; she smiled, she knew Isidoro. My recorder's small light picked up her voice from off the sand. The purple star beside her eye hid in the hand she brought up from her lap. Her daughter, eyes of a dove, alabaster grace, walked into her arms. "Is it difficult here?" I began, as if she knew I knew neither of us was at home. The light of my machine stared at her, and then a voice off the surface of a blade—"I know you!"—tossed across the courtyard. Even as he strode toward me, her voice dropped. He was a tall man in black bathing trunks, and his face was familiar from the tavern where I used to drink and had a home. She will not need to work at Cantina Ra Sol until he flies north. I bet myself the star beside her eye could fit his ring. Improbable story, my townsman guarding my refugee. "She's no refugee." His name was Joe. He thought I was some newspaper, though my recorder had turned to awkward stone.

When my bags were checked, the tape marked "Rosario"
fell to the floor. Her mouth twitched when he spoke, and she
bowed her head. He was lying to protect her, but her eyes,
down a long gun barrel, were firing at me; on a street a rooster
spat a curse and then she fled, pulse of a slim vein in her neck. I
bathed in the Perfume River. I have drowned. He knew
the bigoted war's moon, the secrets in our male hearts, this guy
Joe, drifty ex-Viet marine.

　　I stopped inside the church before the children's rosary
the night of Last *Piñada*. Light hugged the ceiling. Christ above
the altar, head bent, ragged beard, dangled his arms to his thighs.
In lightning he drooped his hands from copper nails, the guide
book says. Candles glitter the spike in his foot. Caught in empty
embrace halfway off the cross on his way to the tomb, he is the
sleepwalker no one bothers to wake. I came west to look for my
so-called self, and south just to look. But I've come here because
they walk right past me and I'm afraid to go like any other
tourist at the border. I want someone now to ask me why I came
here, why I'm on this or any side of a border, but everyone on
earth is in the street, and all I see are their backs as they hurry
out of sight.

　　A new family has taken the room down the hall. Two
women, three tiny girls, and two watchful boys. Past midnight I
walk out on the porch to find the Dipper. It pours the same
black. When I step under it, I feel more North American, hitching
rides in either direction. As the oldest girl, about nine years old,
walks toward me, her hair long and stringy, and lifts her stare
from my sunburned legs to my face, I'm embarrassed as if I
were found too far south. "*Hola!*" I say the one word I'm almost
always sure of quietly for fear of waking Emiliano who blurts a
cackle in his sleep. She smiles, missing two teeth. With the
children I have learned some of the language. She skips away
toward her room and the family. But I would give her sweets,

toys, anything to know what country they have come from, how far have they fled, how long have they been on the road in their dusty blue Volkswagen bug down on Avenida Vera Cruz. The tape is blank in my machine. While she still smiles, I ask, *"De donde eres tu?"* Where are you from? Those eyes of the small girls, always such a militant dark, stare past me, large new pesos. She may be surprised that I sit down on the red cane chair to talk. *"No se... No se ... ,"* she says before stepping though the door. I don't know . . . I don't know.

AT ANY MOMENT

"Those who do not remember history are condemned to repeat it."
— George Santayana

In the overstuffed chair of the hotel lobby, Alonso rises when he sees me and comes to the glass doors. Dark midnight streets ring with cries, screams, small wars, betrayals, the rush of First Avenue traffic and drunken Second Avenue crowds. This afternoon we met in his lawyer's office and spoke about the military in his country, and survivors he calls brothers. In late night combat zones I anticipate being shoved, someone yelling or getting stabbed right before me. I walk rigidly alongside Alonso who is comfortable; he greets everyone, those with scars across the cheek, thin faces of Makah, or those like him fleeing genocide. He tells me to wait at the tavern door while he looks around, so I sit with my small pack. A waitress tells a large Indian to leave before he sits. He is drunk and stumbles away. A man at the bar is talking to himself. Very tall, and formally dressed in scraps of two or three suits, pants too short. He has swollen ankles and sips coffee as if at school, a ripped paper bag by his feet. The lawyer said those not in church sanctuary programs have a double problem on the streets; they are "a refugee on a refugee." Educated Latinos and Indios from families which never prepared them, not only learn to live in a strange land, but to live a vagrant street life.

When Alonso returns shaking his head, I follow him out, relieved he found no one to interview; now I can get back on the bus. As far as I can tell, I am the only middle-class white man out tonight. Nonplussed, Alonso takes me to a noisier place

41

filled with mostly young people, black or Indian. At one table the men seem drunk. One woman is older, the other young and pretty. I am introduced as someone from a newspaper. I nod, yes, I would like to talk to you, but I'm sorry, I do not speak Spanish, and you speak little English. Alonso, who speaks English well, will interpret. They are willing to go out and talk. When we get up to leave and say goodbye to the women, the older one gives me an unfathomable smirk.

As we walk along, Alonso says a message at the hotel informed him his girlfriend is coming from Raymond; she's Makah, and she'll travel far inland to see him. He pays rent by going to the studio of an art buyer and sculpting as many soapstone figurines as he can in a day; he makes enough to cover a week's rent. He is the only one who has a room. No one at the hotel may have visitors, so his "brothers" can't use the room at all. If he could make more money, he would rent an apartment.

Of the other three, Luis speaks English with difficulty. We are going to a park overlooking the waterfront. Eduardo and Raul have their radio and they dance. They are quite young, and Luis, who is energetic, says maybe we will have to fight the group of rowdy white teenagers at the end of the park. I steer them to a table far from the noisy party. My attention is focused on Luis as he tells his story. Rosario and Raul drift off, and I worry I did not hear each one's story. Alonso explains tactfully they are going off to sell the radio. Luis lives on the streets by stealing because he has no other way to survive; none of them except Alonso can get a job or *La Migra* will catch them. "Do you want to go back to your country ever?" He shrugs. "No, I don't want to go back, not now. I want . . . ." He has to think all this out as he says it. "I want to . . . you know . . . get a girl . . . get married . . . have a house . . . and a job." I am reminded of the distinction our government makes between political and economic refugees, and immediately I place Luis in the latter category, until he says, "If I go back, I will be killed."

He was in the army, and later with the guerrillas. I ask did he participate in military searches? No, he did not. Did he kill anybody, anyone of his own age, his own people? He doesn't answer. Why did he leave? He finally saw what was going on and couldn't do what was ordered. Alonso remembers seeing a skull; the head had been drenched in acid. Luis had his own images which did not let him continue in the military. But he would have been a child. Yes, he was young. Death Squads, however, shook him up; he stopped wearing his uniform, he dropped out, stayed home. Once he was on the street when two soldiers saw him; one had been a classmate. They were going to arrest him because they knew he was supposed to be in the army. The one he knew told him to go home. "'Be careful, go away.' Then when I was gone, staying at my girlfriend's house," he grins, "my mother said they came and searched. They were looking for me." He left home, and for a short time fought as a guerrilla. I get the impression that while fighting with the *Guerrilleros*, he came and went in his own home. He fled the country because his mother believed Death Squads would kill him, and his girlfriend was worried. So he got out.

Santiago speaks as one who has lived there all his life, yet he was born and raised in the Southwest. He is about to defend a refugee seeking political asylum, the first such case in the Pacific Northwest. Distinctions between "economic" and "political" are meaningless. Someone fleeing for his or her life may seek a higher income. You talk to many of them and they tell you they're here to make money, support the family, send money home. Ask if they'd die if they went home, they shrug, they don't know. Do they know anybody who was killed? Yes. Would they be killed? They don't know, to be honest. They might be. Why would they? They don't know, they shrug. Why were the others killed? They don't know. There was no reason—you were walking along the street one night with so and so, next day they're dead. You worry. You were seen walking. Was he in the union? Yes. No. Maybe. The military might say unions are subversive, so they kill everyone in unions. They turn up dead on the roads, found without heads, killed in public places. Then they may think it's students. The same to the students. They launch terror campaigns so everyone stays away from unions, students, whatever group is put upon. It's someone suspected of being a sympathizer, or a Jew, or in the union, or Catholic, students,. We cannot understand this; it has never happened to us. Then the next step: they forget labels, take out people indiscriminately . . . someone you were talking to, someone who looked like you. Someone in your age group; if you're seventeen to thirty-five and not in the military, you're a guerrilla. You cannot be non-political. Most of them in this country are 22, 23, and 24. You wonder if they get older. Courts may try to find reasons for killings, but the reason is there are no reasons! Anyone can be killed, any time, and in a frighteningly inhuman way. Torture. Brutality. It is a program of induced mass hallucination, constant random death. Our courts do not provide a category for randomness. You are in danger either because of race, religion, or class. It is not enough you are between seventeen and thirty-five and everyone you know is killed and you don't know why. You can't be absolutely sure you will be killed if you return to your country. *El Tecolote*, in San Francisco, said that out of 1,100 who applied for asylum this year, sixty-two were granted. It's considerably less, though. I know of only three who received asylum. How can courts give asylum to protect someone from repression by a government already certified free of human-rights violations? It would seem a question a judge should consider, but he is sworn not to. Each case must be proved life-threatening. Courts exist to defend current policy. They have no class in common; there is no religious persecution or racial difference with their killers. The simple fact is men in the prime of life, the age of soldiers, are killed for no reason and a nationwide terror strangles the country. A fear or randomness that at any moment can wipe out anyone. We might say we're all in danger here. We could be blown apart by an attack, but *there* it is every moment, it is now, and we in North America can't believe it happens. If we were able to believe in the reality of a nuclear bomb or an attack on American soil, how could we live our lives? Only in fear could we continue our routines if we had in our minds pictures of soldiers tossing babies into the air— catching them on bayonets. I don't want to believe it. How could we believe people have ripped open the bellies of pregnant women, removed fetus and, inserted the heads of fathers? Our contemporaries, maybe fellow citizens, yet so different our worst dreams can't describe.

Imagine if one twelfth of the population were exiled, and sought asylum in another country. Our culture would be destroyed. Our growth as a society would stop. Arts and sciences would be state controlled. We would return to fascist art that replaced freer, livelier periods like the Weimar Republic. This situation has happened. One twelfth of their country's population, five hundred thousand, is in our country. More have left: artists, writers, painters, engineers, students, lawyers. The university shut down and is inhabited by the National Guard. Their country will be retarded socially and culturally, a country already underdeveloped made more so by our government's collusion with theirs. Churches that give sanctuary are doing an incredible servic, but engineering students became winos— artists, law students are drunks, bums, thieves, and some just can't hack it with the churches. They're given a place to stay. They're tired, maybe they've been running, hiding, they're thinking about their families, not able to send money. A nice bottle of wine's locked in a cabinet at the church. Next day three drunken refugees on the floor. So they have to go. On the street they face getting picked up and turned over to Immigration. They could be sent back as illegal or undocumented workers. Or arrested as vagrants. At home they will probably

45

be killed; they're always in hiding, a class of persecuted people without a name.

Alejandra seemed more inclined to continue office work, and with frequent phone calls there was little time to talk. Three men came in, obviously clients, to pick up forms. They spoke no English, and laughed.

She left her country, and, caught crossing the border, spent six months in a Texas jail. Why did she leave? Some problem with her job at the phone company. She came from a comfortable family with little to fear from the government. The war made it impossible to live normally. Santiago had spoken of young men in danger. Well-dressed, sophisticated, clerical in manner, she would not have been a guerrilla. What precipitated her leaving was the refusal by some of her co-workers to obey orders. One was arrested and tortured. The order was to monitor phone calls. Following arrest and torture, she and the rest of the workers still refused to record phone calls. They were threatened. She kept her job a while longer, but going to work became dangerous and she had to leave. Then six months in Texas. Horrible, as you may imagine. Texas jails on the border are crowded with refugees. Conditions are oppressive and unsanitary. When she got out, she came to Seattle and worked for the Refugee Legal Service. She applied for political asylum because she herself had been threatened before leaving.

When she refused to cooperate, she had no recourse because the military runs the telephone company, the bank, and the university. They control buying and selling commodities. To buy groceries you must go to the door of the store and order through a slit. The grocer will pass things, but is supervised. It is a military state to an extent we can't imagine. Refugees from her country flee for their lives; deporting them is sending them to Hitler. There is a process of advancement in the army starting as second lieutenant, first lieutenant, and so forth. You become general, then minister. A process of political appointments wherein one officer appoints another to administer a department. A minister controls departmental resources. Officers look forward to ministries because the military alone provides no economic base from which to operate. All coffee plantations, for example, are controlled by the oligarchy. An officer can become involved in a ministry like the Institute of Agrarian Reform. The ministry is the recipient of economic aid from America, and controls that aid and departmental resources. The result is graft.

Many think the U.S. initiated the Institute of Agrarian Reform in 1979, but the Institute existed long before, operated by the military. One way the military became rich was to overprice land already developed through economic aid usurped by the oligarchy. The military used capital allotted to the Institute, paid land owners millions, and got kickbacks. Economic aid we send goes to colonels' pockets. They don't have a natural economic base, so in war they protect their interests. They don't care about communist, democrat, socialist, Islamic, Protestant, Catholic. Anyone who tries to create a democratic system is a threat. Each and every member takes part in graft and corruption. In a democracy somebody will have to pay the price for that corruption, and the military will not tolerate that. We train ministers for posts in an attempt to create a system we can control, in which the military will fight to win, fight a more than nine-to-five, no-weekend war. Each officer wants his chance to be rich. Guerrillas win because the military doesn't have the heart for victory. Their officers are itinerants. After a dictator falls, his cronies and lackeys join the army of another country's dictator. This is what produced the unbalanced economy. A country of six million, with the highest death rate by starvation after Bangladesh. The poor can only do seasonal work on plantations. They live on one hundred thirty-five dollars a year. Picking up the gun is the end of patience. They're through watching children die one by one. It's not from ideology or fundamentalism. I've met only a few who can explain the fundamentals. It's hunger, anger, lack of hope that makes an ordinary person pick up a gun.

Alonso likes it here, but yes he would go back. He is waiting for the guerrillas to win so he can return. When Santiago declared they are turning people away because they don't have enough guns, and two hundred thousand out of five hundred thousand refugees would go back and fight, Alonso said yes, yes, I would do that. Alejandra said yes, I will go back. Oh yes, I will go back if I have a gun.

He has a wife and a daughter. They are with another man. "I had to go through that, too." A refugee on a refugee. When his girlfriend comes to him, she cannot go to his room because of the hotel rules.

He tries not to be stopped by city police. He walks within crosswalks, waits for lights. Once he was arrested and given a fine. The fine has his name on it, all he has to identify himself. Around two hundred of his brothers and he have many problems. One-third of restaurant workers in Washington, D.C., are from his home. "We are all over the country, and we have many problems being here, just living, and staying alive."

Luis steals like other street people, sells things the way Eduardo and Raul went to sell the radio. They have no choice. He has a place to stay tonight, if he can make the last bus, then sleep on a floor. Usually, he doesn't have this. Many refugees spend the night walking, then in daylight sleep in the park beside a bottle. Walking away from our bench, we see a security guard talking to another man. Luis and Alonso don't look at him; they walk along the edge beside the locked booths of the outdoor market. Luis quickens his pace and walks ahead. Turning, he shakes hands, says, "Adios," walks fast again, stops suddenly, turns, scoops up a small cube of watermelon from the street and laughs.

PASSENGERS

Moving along at about fifteen miles an hour, the engine passed us. As I strapped on my pack, it reached the turn at the end of the yard and picked up speed—a long train, plenty of cars. We were in a place where the tracks made a "Y" not ten feet in front of us, not enough room to run alongside, watch the train, and avoid stumbling and being crushed; at three feet high, the switch light would be easy to hit and break a leg. I almost did a week earlier, dropping from a slow train in the dark. To add to the problem, only enclosed grain cars with small platforms and a ladder would do us any good. It was difficult to think and too loud to shout. A grain car was coming up fast, so I grabbed the handrail and took a few running steps, but something in my will didn't click on, and I couldn't step up the ladder. I let go, tossing on our jug, with the only water we'd see for miles. We kept running—Finn and I were between the moving cars and uncoupled units of the next train—and we hoped not to hit anything behind us with our packs. Finn grabbed a grain car ladder, but hoisting himself up, he banged his knee and crawled up its steps. He yelled back: "Don't try it . . . It's moving too fast!" More cars passed and for a second I saw the two refugees on the other side of the train. I had a pang of worry for their distressed faces; they looked as if they'd never done this before, but it was either worry about them and be left behind, or get myself up one of these ladders. Another grain car came up the line, and I had a better feel for its speed. Without thinking I took hold of a handrail and ran with the train, took one step and I was lifted up. Finn was waving from a few cars up the line. Pulling myself up the ladder, I realized I hadn't completely intended to get on; the train had just pulled me. Down the line of cars one man hopped on, a hand helping him, and farther back one more was running beside the car, tossing on his gear. The train was moving very fast.

*

In Yakima, on dry brown hills and sunny streets, crisp and frail, leaves drop from trees in their first autumn the color of summer oranges and reds like the hide of a fox. The frost is bright at dawn, a crisp chill before sunset, elevation over 2,000 feet. The Japanese Current in Puget Sound has made me forget true cold. My idea of the Northwest has been insular all these years. More than mist, fog, rain, herons, and wool hats, this weather, a cold you can see coming, can feel in the excited citizens—that is, the whites, Anglos who talk casually yet always of snow—must be cold indeed for refugees from even farther away than me. According to the cable station on the fuzzy motel TV, the migrant population is so great at apple harvest that churches and growers are concerned over the high number of illegal aliens. Many kids in my classes slip easily out of English in drafting a poem. I told a seventh-grade girl to go ahead and write in her first language, but the girl behind her said she'd better not. As visiting poet, I whispered revolt in the ears of the young and met an old response; language maintains its burden of control.

I keep remembering the faces of the three refugees and Ruben who joined us just as the train left the yard. One is more clear than the others, more anxious to communicate when we make our funny attempts to mime and signal. I learned nothing for certain, but he seemed to grasp my meaning, though he could have been answering entirely different questions, those I should have asked. What happened to make you leave your home? How did you become displaced? Did you leave together? Why? What was it? What did you see? What did you know? Who did you leave? What happened to your families? They will tell me they

50

left the border four days ago. They will not tell where. I might not recognize them here among the crowds—in the market near school, on the street, by the railroad yard, at the orchard. The Yakima harvest was their destination.

We expected to be in Seattle that same night, but twenty-five miles out of Portland, our train pulled off the main line to circle a grain elevator beside the highway where drivers cruised in utter silence. I could have hitchhiked with less difficulty. Before we were sidetracked, the Seattle ride had ended. It was a place where other trains wouldn't stop. Anything coming would pass us like a dirty shirt, as Monty the Commie Hobo used to say. Finn and I jumped off while the train slowed down, and we yelled to the others to jump before it got them too far off course.

*

Their faces up the mainline where there will be no slow trains. In the center is Ruben, an older man. Despite the weariness in their eyes, the three others are just boys. Ruben speaks English well, although he told us no, his *ingles* "ease no gude." He had climbed aboard when our train made a stop; running out of the bushes, he joined Finn and me on the platform of a grain car. We were going at a good clip when he asked if we'd like a drink. It was noon and hot and my nose was already burning. Ruben wore a heavy army field jacket, the shirt open under it, his chest smeared with sweat and dirt. He produced a dark green bottle. The smile of one who knows some things well passed over his face. All his front teeth were missing, his mouth dark as any tunnel. The *Night Train* label glowered in black letters at the top of an engine's diesel plume. Almost every wino we met wanted us to drink from a bottle of *Night Train*, just one hit, no more. I remembered creatures in my worst hangovers, so I declined. He took a gulp and slid the little engine back inside his shirt. What a smile! Someone gave him the bottle and jacket because he was heading north, his first time on trains, first visit to Seattle.

51

He would go to a mission to get something to eat, and figure from there where to go. Maybe he would pick the fruit; he didn't know. Three others on this train, I told him, were on their way to pick the fruit.

Next time the train stopped they joined us on the grain car's platform. Ruben and they exchanged rapid questions: where you from? Where you going? Do you know Jesus Montejo? Gabriella Soto-Batista? Yolanda or Vernonica Espinoza or Zavala? They spoke the same language. Wherer did they come from? As they talked, I kept listening for the distinct sound naming their country, but I heard nothing like it. I was curious whether they would try to hide where they were from. How did they determine whom to trust? They told me without hesitation, yet I gave them no reason to trust me. They didn't immediately trust Ruben, but I couldn't tell why. Maybe they'd had a bad experience with someone like him. Maybe they heard stories about aliens who might, for no reason at all, turn them in, or maybe some darker instinct was at work. I couldn't tell by their accents or clothing, but Ruben on that train platform had a troubled look on his face. He could tell by words. "Dose mains . . . they not safe!" The words of one of their Goodwill T-shirts, scrawled in red above bleak toothy faces—"Hunger, Running"— didn't identify or give me any meaning. Ruben will leave as I will, walking off to let them escape. He will walk off toward First Avenue in Seattle with a light skip—Skid Road, Pioneer Square, grass, jug, sun, and his dark smile.

When the one trying to make Ruben believe they were from his own country glanced at me, his eyes faded and he looked at his feet again. He may have been asking me not to give them away. He hadn't come to trust this Ruben yet, but when they had finished and were smiling at some last joke, when they were looking at the world fly by over grinding screaming metal, Ruben leaned toward me, against the car wall as it rocked, and told me, although he stared straight ahead, in a voice just above a whisper: "They are desperate men," his thin lips in a bad smile. "They are not legal," shaking his head, looking at his own shoes.

These faces come before me at a café window as I sit and watch drivers navigate snow, where snow forever falls. Faces of illegal men, crumbs of the empire—less: dust has fallen beneath a floor, a fine powder chased onto grinding tracks. Only by forbidding asylum to children, born losers in a crowd of losers, does empire cohere; for no place in its vast territories can appear to threaten the lives of citizens, unless of course such a threat lets us tighten the grip on some wealth we didn't remember until now: oil, uranium, hemispheric control of labor; it was salt with Gandhi; our own weapons inadvertently aimed our way from North Korea.

They have their heads together like old friends, Ruben instructing them in what he knows of hiding, but he can't go with them. He would make it easier, since he speaks English, but he can't bring himself to say yes. They must hide even from the dawn because when they show their faces America looks up; like these workers in a caboose awaiting a train to take them to Seattle, sipping coffee on the air buoyant with the smell of hills where they first went hiding, *fincas* where they worked. Sometimes when the train slows enough, they jump off to change cars or run beside it. They are athletes in the purest sense; they compete against thought. Nothing can matter now—something is lost and something is coming. Only to live this perfectly, to complete this, matters.

When they are before us we tell them we have spoken to the engineer. We have walked a quarter mile of heat from where our train was dropped off. He spoke to us with unusual recklessness, as if he might lose his job, but he'd tell us anyway goddammit! "Be careful of these fuckin' trains. I can't tell ya not to, but this is a dangerous way to go. Guy could lose a arm, or a leg just like that an' that train don't care. Why, you could turn aroun' wrong an' it'd take a damn head right off an' keep goin'.

So be careful. These cars over here're all goin' ta Seattle. Twenny-one of 'em. Ain't a boxcar on 'em. They'll be takin' outa here any minute. Well, good luck!"

We know all this about the danger—that's why we came. Unlike hunted men who can't return to countries where having fled is cause for death, or who can't travel freely because the lack of credentials leads to the same thing, we were men whose lives just didn't have enough danger. Who sought this railroad adventure freely never doubting we'd have soft beds and warm meals to return to—mailboxes bearing our names. Except for the language barrier, this was all that set us apart from the three refugee boys trying to slip through our country. That and the country itself, trains booming out steel symphonies and a man standing above us gazing over all five like a land baron with bad grammar, issuing warnings that pertain as much to property rights as to fierce machinery that freights the nation's arrogant assumptions from one border to the next.

There was nothing. Twenty-one cars and each offered a rail of steel a half-foot wide without platform. Ruben rode one like that the night before we met. He took on that impossible I-beam and held tight to the rail, afraid to fall asleep. Though he'd sworn he'd never ride one again, here he was. "I have no choice. I have to take this train with them." His funny smile was only half-formed when he rolled his head back and forth. I tried to explain how dangerous it was, but they just gave me a curious look. "Dangerous! Dangerous!"Trying to make the word stick. I wasn't going to have my chance to ask questions, unless I made them stay. The train was about to start. Couldn't I get Ruben to translate quickly? I had to keep them from leaving. They should not do this. But how bad has it been already? The dangers they have seen are impossible to calculate through their calm smiles, and now through their handshakes and waves. I imagine their effort to get here. They have come in on a tide wearing the clothes they have, nothing in their pockets, some money stuffed in the toe of a tennis shoe. Who knows how long they were moving north. They might have told of people tortured, who fled and were sent back by Immigration.

But I don't want to ask. I don't want to see the eager one's ineffable look into some well he stands at where he hears voices of those he can't name. He has taken the rose from the Colonel's desk and the dark hand is reaching for it. He was in the street and he saw the man with no head. He was at his job and he saw the head. He was in church and the blood fell on his bare ankles. He was in the bathroom and the voice rushed in the water. He was with his lover and the tongue ceased to move. He was having dinner and the flesh stinking in the yard made him go hungry. He was praying and the screams were terrible.

I watched him climb to the top of the train where he waved. When they all mounted the car and found footing, the train started and with a grin he held up the slip of paper I gave him with the lawyer's phone number. I didn't know the words for "good luck." I wanted to say I knew what they were fleeing, but not even that. In that moment I was only aware of smiling, while I watched the immense canyon between us widen.

II

I admit I was the first to wake
inside the long dormitory.
I was ready for moonlight.
During Easter Midnight Mass
in a lily's shadow Father Cardillo
strained on a ladder of Gregorian notes,
his voice almost falsetto,
passionate as a man in love.
The year turned off-course,
from long nights in northern woods
to brilliant dawn. Later, when the sun knit
the skirt of pine to the window,
I slipped back into chapel
to beg I too be lifted, as he was.
I waited for the voice, I admit that.
I waited for the perfume of a lily
to saturate these clothes.
Shouts of school boys rose from a field.
A wren broke its heart singing.
Jets echoed off the chapel roof.
When I heard earth whistle in space,
I ran down the tilted hall.

MY FIRST POEM

Nailed to the sloped ceiling of my so-called garrett outside Porter Square was a banner on which I'd scrawled in my own best script the Russian proverb, "Eat Bread & Salt and Speak the Truth." The walls were turquoise mottled by shadows, a bare bulb at the peak of the Spartan white peak of ceiling; a desk lamp, reading lamp, a wax mound of candle beside the bed. Until three or four in the morning, the silver percolator pumped espresso, snow four inches up the window. A typewriter, a notebook, or some desperate lined paper may have been on the desk, bearing my imitations of Ezra Pound's imitations of Greek poems. Between 1968 and 1970, although the Vietnam War was raging, I had no television and didn't read newspapers. I kept up by attending protest marches, benefit concerts, or once a picnic with the SDS, but only to meet women. The world of current events was less interesting than the Pound biography my friend Mark had given me. He worked in the only bookstore open late nights in Harvard Square; he'd begun recommending poets on my second purchase of cheap novels. He may have seen me browse the poetry section, and suggested Pound, later providing me with a course of contemporary poets. Stacked next to my blue overstuffed chair were *Cantos, Selected Poems*, and *ABC of Reading*. That winter all I did was read Pound, skip class, walk around Harvard Square at dawn, and smoke butts from the gutter.

That was two years after they kicked me out of the seminary. Or I left. Whichever interpretation surfaced from time to time, what's apparent now is I agreed with the priests: I should return to "the world." During my last months, entrusted with keys to the sacristy, I unlocked the communion wine and sipped from a small glass, my back to the tabernacle, staring into darkness at one or two in the warm summer mornings of Tampa Bay, where I thought God was now an enlarged challenge to forgive.

Although responsible for the "Church Latin" of *Liber Usualis*, I knew the Classics nonetheless. Had Pound demanded the *Aeneid* in Latin, I'd have been ready, but his *ABC of Reading* said a poet should at least have read Homer in Greek and Dante in Italian. This impressed me more than G.K. Chesterton's quip: a gentleman should have forgotten his Greek. I'd failed to be admitted to Homer in the seminary, defaulting to New Testament Greek, disappointed not to study with my sharpest classmates the *Iliad* and *Odyssey*. Yet familiarity with dead languages, and an additional year of Italian, led me to "Dante, The Duecento," a course which the University of Massachusetts conducted in Italian (a detail I'd overlooked in the catalog, to the chagrin of my classmates, and sometimes to the professor's when in bad Italian, then English, scoring points as I saw it, for erudition, I recounted snippets of Church history and half-baked poetics). I hired a tutor to practice Italian, and translated a selection of cantos from throughout *Commedia* on lined paper I never respected enough to keep.

These versions never struck me as poetry, nor did my syllable-by-syllable Pound imitations. Translating Dante was more familiar than any aspect of what I supposed was my apprenticeship. At times the text gave up splinters of Dante's vision of divine light in the *Paradiso*, but I worked up no more than a sincere enthusiasm for the drudgery; from Dante's vulgate I made no new poem. Maybe motive separates one's early work from poetry. Practice poems are translations of a kind. As a student for whom school was primarily the act of looking up words in dictionaries, acquiring familiarity with convoluted structures, parsing obscure verbs in his mother tongue, I thought "being a poet" natural. I dressed for it, parading in black cape, high boots, white fur hat, and hitchhiked Mass Ave. I smoked *Galois* like a good existentialist, carried poems in an army surplus

60

knapsack, ready to throw down at the first raised eyebrow. I was obsessed, but with form, the "mantle of the poet," as someone phrased it years later—the poet prince handing his famous cape to a successor. I had the barest inkling of that untamed spirit which imbues words we think to call poetry.

When poets visit classrooms, they are often asked: "When did you write your first poem?" It's a more explicit question than, "How old were you when you started to write?" That one always seems more the asker setting notorious expectations: Did I start too young? Am I working at the right pace? Is it already too late? My answer has usually been unsatisfying, perhaps I hurry through. Some poets, I understand, began as children, and received encouragement from parents, friends, and teachers. I always stop after saying that when I was fifteen I wrote a religious poem for a feast day in high school, the junior seminary. A spring evening, all the boys attending the artistic celebrations in black suits on folding chairs near the statue of the Virgin Mary, I read in a high voice in the middle of 150 acres of birdsong and Massachusetts crickets, a mimicry of marching Victorian meters in aabba rhyme; an historical poem in which the Pope prays to the Virgin because Turks were about to invade Rome, but then camped in Hungary for 150 years. It was a horrible thing, and although first attempts must not always be failures, mine deserved the clammy applause that followed, just as I deserved a ribbing from Joe Beyes, an upperclassman— "Aha! The young Robert Frost." He flattered me by even speaking to me, a miserable sophomore. I deserved ridicule because I wrote a poem, and had the nerve to read it. I deserved it because where I came from, a neighborhood not known for its contributions to the Arts, poetry was for sissies. I tried again at twenty, also religious, bad Eliot, and lifted that forbidden wine to my lips in Florida, and didn't write again for three years.

Abbreviating the story to give a functional answer, dates and trite biographical information which doesn't amount to much, I notice the questioner become shy, if a little horrified.

But it's a lie, because that was not my first poem. Nor did I write it in those two years in Cambridge. But something came about then, something woke up, shook off the snow, and opened its eyes. A year before, I was staying at the "Y" in Pawtucket, Rhode Island, working at a toy factory, and I'd written a simple description that employed words I never used before. Not the whole piece, but a few of the lines startled me, so I tried more. Under the desk lamp in Cambridge, my notebook open to lines about a rose on my shelf turning black, I wrote, "A swag of velvet on a spindling shaft" without knowing what "swag" meant. Not the first poem, but the first insight, which I can even date. The rest was in waiting, but I didn't know that as I worked fiercely at syllables of *Cantos* or the *Purgatorio*, pausing to notice how my mouth felt to read Dante aloud. The mystery of real poetry lay in imitation and translation.

A new fervor took the place of religion, fed by books Mark suggested, and poetry journals, among them an issue he'd edited. After glossy Pound books, I wondered where the Moderns were in the college library of the seminary, which let me read only Frost and Thomas. Frost's depth of feeling held me even in high school when I studied the *Complete Poems*; Thomas's life opened my eyes, and his recorded readings, the turns of language, compact meanings and range of music, offered me an early model. Eliot's *Collected Poems*, roughly as slim as Thomas's, did not elicit discussion in our seminary about the effects of the first half of the 20th century on poetry. Books to fill in the gaps by these poets and others were out of reach behind the "amber curtain," restricted to seminarians with research projects and required permissions.

So Mark's journals became my introduction to small-press editions of selections that barely broke even: thin volumes on rag paper, or bark, handset in limited editions, mimeographed, stapled, handed out in the Square in the morning. Or low-budget offset in black-and-white and department money. It was how those Moderns saw things; eke out enough to find readers, have friends review, promote you wildly. In Mark's apartment were stacks of books, magazines, manuscripts, and framed signed portraits of poets I didn't know. At Black Mountain School, Olson replaced Director Buckminster Fuller, whose reputation even I was aware of, and Creeley, Duncan, Levertov, and many others were instructors. He showed me poems by Robert Kelly in letterpress books, an issue of *Swallow* with Creeley, and an inscribed copy of one of Duncan's poems. I read *The Maximus Poems, Projective Verse,* and *Maximus* again.

Mark was from Alabama and the sound of an Olson line or Kelly poem, made even more exotic by his dialect, helped me grasp those heady abstractions; I was raised with broad Boston Irish, and the thick Italian accents of priests. Even in the wild suburbs of Florida I'd never come across a genuine Southern twang. The crackle of those syllables in Kelly or Creeley made me recognize how poetry sounds when it's not just in my head. He read theatrically, and had a slant on things that left me suspect. "Did you know 'gabardine' comes from 'Garbo'?" He was going through a divorce, picking up taxi work as well as hours in the bookstore, and drinking pretty hard. He may have been drunk when I took him apartment hunting, and he told me from the bathroom, "Never rent an apartment 'tll you try the toilet, and bring a good book of poems." I thought of all the books I would have to carry, as I traipsed empty hardwood floors, assuming I'd be tapped for the move. I went on having beers with him in downtown bars beside bookstores and universities. I never met his wife, nor did he talk about her. I'm not sure if he had children. It seems he mentioned the custody struggle forced him to take the second job; he stopped and honked from his cab once on Boylston Street, and above the busy traffic, recited a poem.

Across from my attic room in the house I shared with four graduate students lived Ivory who, when asked where he was from, always answered "Brooklyn" with a British accent, and who rarely gave information about himself. He was married and had a child; they lived in Paris, but he would stay here until

63

he had a doctorate from Harvard and could work for the Kenyan government. Ivory never appeared to study—he had no desk in his room. Two years earlier I'd been a student in an environment where study was a certain posture at a desk with drawers containing your own pens, paper, and written work—one of three hundred in a hall the size of two football fields (the last hurrah of giant seminaries in America), so I had a distinct advantage in judging what was intellectual activity and what was not. He had only the bed and one or two overstuffed chairs, where I would sit occasionally and tell him about Dante or complain about my struggle with the language. He disapproved of poetry; it was less significant than history or philosophy. He had a lot to say about Vietnam and activities of Congress. Not opinions on Congressional prudence, his comments fit our government into a trend he called the Revolution. Yet he didn't attend rallies or marches in Cambridge and Boston, didn't project interest in changing society.

The Revolution was a new concept for me. None of my seminary classes prepared me to look at the universe as social history. I had perhaps a different education than priests and nuns who became politically outspoken. It was not my inclination to think of poetry, hence the universe, as anything but a metaphysical entity. Thomas Aquinas taught me that. I was not prepared for a world not antagonistic, yet Ivory, when I ran into him and his girlfriend at a laundromat, gave me a glimpse of the utopia he envisioned. "Won't it be better," he asked, "when we leave our clothes washing because we know a neighbor will put them in the dryer?" I don't know if he or I was in a hurry to be somewhere else at the time. "And when we come back, the clothes will be folded?" He was smiling, being mischievous. I wasn't sure if he was mocking Revolution, expressing an ideal, or trying to get me to do his laundry. It was also new for me to be around someone who was not white. My Boston Irish childhood, and seven years in the seminary (ages fourteen to twenty-one in priest's cassock, a blackout of puberty) had offered few encounters with cultures unlike mine, and the notorious racism of the times had a stranglehold on Dorchester and South Boston where I grew up. To live close to a black man, especially one more European than American, who asked many questions, provoked me to tether my answers on the strange identity of cultural tour guide. I explained human behavior as acceptable to rationalize motives of politicians or elucidate meanings of sentences he quoted from Marx or Engels. Ivory's answers were equally determinist, offering inevitable social change. I failed to recognize that he was planting by Socratic questioning a course in dialectical materialism, an ideology for which I was fertile ground.

He gave me a copy of John Stuart Mills's *On Liberty*, but I couldn't get past page five, deterred by dense language, or maybe *Paradiso* was more to my liking. We went to a lecture given by Herbert Marcuse, whose books Ivory was steadily working through. Marcuse was a provocative speaker, instructive, funny and rational, and yet for me the details of the Revolution were less important than the way he trilled the letter 'r' in "radical." We attended Ayn Rand's lecture as well. Rand, who was belligerent, a philosopher for whom *will* and *self* determined success, asked the room at large if "hippies" wanted us to smash our washing machines and dishwashers, after we struggled so hard to get them, and move back onto the land to scrub old cloth on river stones. Many young women in the audience were dressed for such a life, though we were in the middle of a harsh metropolitan winter; the image of them kneeling on the banks was so appealing, I resolved to leave Boston soon.

As Ivory led me to the contradictory views of Marcuse and Rand, he opened a window onto philosophies of social justice. My attempts at poetry began to include people more than the gulls and dunes and cigarettes I'd been shoveling into disjointed stanzas. Yet I couldn't abandon my metaphysical search; it was the oxygen I breathed; the universe had meaning at a level I insisted was mysterious. The mystery I dwelt within, to use

Biblical phrasing, was a version of the theories of Teilhard de Chardin, the mystic French anthropologist-priest. Proposing them without imprimatur, he contended that matter defines events and history more than do struggles for power; existence itself, not interpretation, was the basis for the spiritual life I assumed as the medium of all poets. Contemplative lives led to poetry. The existential experience had been depicted in the seminary when one of the brothers stood up in philosophy class, speechless, clutching the back of a chair. He ran his hands along the smooth grain of oak, eyes wide, unable to speak, until almost choking, he managed to say "This . . ." and then a long pause, the class stunned he could say no more, "This . . . is!" We reached a consensus that the brother had experienced what our professor termed the "Intuition of Being." Such an event in the childhood of Elizabeth Bishop is recorded in her poem, "In the Waiting Room." I hoped to portray Being in poetry, though I couldn't have been conscious of metaphor as distinct from understanding, and now I let social justice sit comfortably with my metaphysical intuitions.

Perhaps the little I understood of Chardin influenced my reading of Olson. To think of *Maximus* as an epic, I had to recognize Olson's metaphors of change in geologic and civilized time. Mark introduced me to Pound and Olson primarily, just as Ivory introduced me to Marcuse and Rand. Marcuse had become something of a mentor for him, as Olson had for Mark. Both Ivory and Mark, a study in opposites, were my own mentors: a black radical philosopher, cool and unassuming, funny and irreverent (on a sailing trip in Maine he told me that if our host, the aging heart surgeon, captain of an eighty-foot schooner, spoke that way to his self-effacing wife again, he'd "knock him upside the haid"—British accent) and a big, white, Southern Baptist with a twang and lisp, a poet and lyrical thinker (he told me "I don't want ideas in my head"—I was stunned. I hadn't learned to wait for the other shoe to drop when Mark made this kind of pronouncement—"I just want images."). So I became a reader of Olson and Marcuse, mentors of mentors. Maybe "model" is the more useful term, since "mentor" has become a verb as well as a job description. Dante, whose mentor led him through Hell and Purgatory, said in *De Monarchia*, "The more closely we copy the great poets, the more correct is the poetry we write." We might quibble over the meaning of the word "copy," but arguing with Dante's interpretation of "correct" might prove hopeless. Mentor, so it happens, was the friend of the family whose form Athena took to teach Telemachus what he must do to become a man—go find your father, kill off these pretenders who waste your resources, seek the truth. It may be that any force guiding those about to take control of their lives, as Athena did with the son of Odysseus, could be called divinely inspired, or at the very least, available for free advice. Luckily or not, people have always dug right in to the project of giving me advice and I've been predisposed to take it, imagining I'd found guidance for my next decision.

Selecting mentors may be compulsive for writers, even those working against the grain. At an open mike in a Seattle coffee shop weeks after the riots in response to the first meeting of the World Trade Organization, many poets found inventive ways to complain about the treatment police gave protestors. Some talked about the WTO as the global oppressor, a term denied with all the imperialist naiveté and vehemence the designated spokespersons could summon for the papers. Those readers and reciters were alike in volume and emphasis, phrasing (influenced by rap in a few cases) and cadence, in vulgarity and downright nastiness. Having participated in many readings around the city, they were friends in a competitive slam, duplicating or out-performing one another's style. Many current poetry magazines adopt and promote a similar range of styles; contributors express like values in styles that have similar limitations. Certainly editorial preference accounts for similarity, but poets often write for particular tastes, so their work will be published in The Bigs. Perhaps similarities arise from workshops where good poetry and what is not are clearly discerned, and where doubt and self-examination are out of place.

The habit of imitation I cultivated in my early attempts at poetry was similar. All I had to do was learn how, and my work could stand alongside those in poetry journals. The role of the poet replaced my identification with the priesthood, yet it was a vocation, intimately connected to training in the spiritual life: rigorous discipline, faith in the existence of a soul, an inclination to believe in the efficacy of poems; like good works in the religious life, poems could change the world. I understood why Yeats dwelt so on the *Spiritus Mundi*, and I replaced religious views with Jung's collective unconscious. Although not everyone approaches poetry in flight from a strict religious background, writing to top our contemporaries, or copy great poets, is a step toward the first poem; yet we may work against our inclination and are easily satisfied, demanding less than the art deserves.

Come spring I was putting the finishing touches on what I thought of as "the long poem." There was a strong influence of the sea, a familiar setting, images triggered by sailing the Maine coast; one evening while I was seasick over the heart surgeon's starboard rail, Ivory looped a line around my wrist to ensure they could haul me out of the still harbor should I slip overboard in nauseated sleep. Something violent and complaining was in that writing, descriptions of islands and vessels Ahab or a similar figure passed on his way to an encounter in the opposite direction. *The Divine Comedy*, Pound's *Cantos*, and *Maximus Poems*—although I'd read only a smattering of each—I took to be my influences. I wouldn't have said "models" at the time, because I wasn't intentionally imitating: this was all my own. Yet Charles Olson's style—the page as graphic art, the line as breath, and close observations of the coast—had become a template. His and Pound's typical abbreviations and sometimes awkward hyphens, even their humor, had been precursors of the form I assumed. And from Dante I learned to see the world as allegory, or perhaps

I could sustain three lines once in a while. This quilt of stolen devices grew to almost ten double-spaced pages and I was certain there was more.

Mark asked in August if I'd like to go to Gloucester, about an hour and a half north, to visit Olson before he died. He let me know that a friend of his was going to pay his last respects, that it would be good for me to go. Yet I really didn't know who Charles Olson was. In reading him and absorbing the tradition, I was aware of form, but I hadn't spent time with his vision (nor to be truthful, with Pound's and Dante's). I missed the meaning. I couldn't say that Olson became clearer to me. I hadn't imagined looking out his front window onto Gloucester Bay, or at his "Neolithic neighbors." Years later I used a street map to find his house; a helpful pedestrian there guessed he "might have been a painter?" He had neighbors downstairs, on three sides, and the sea in front; Gloucester's fishing history and New England's commerce streamed and sailed and motored past his window. I'll give myself credit for thinking it was a tacky thing to do, pay my respects to a poet I didn't know, though certainly there were reasons I can't recall, something going on that weekend I would have missed; I had never seen anyone close to death except my beloved uncle who was oddly unchanged by the hospital bed. Whatever my reasons, for years I've wished I had gone. Maybe I wanted to avoid intruding. Regardless—banishing altruism and pettiness, as Ayn Rand would have advised because it was a pivotal moment to change my life—I should have witnessed how a great poet dies. "I'm going to hate to leave this Earthly Paradise," he wrote in *Maximus* the year before he died. "Only the divine alone interests me at all."

Nevertheless, I continued my "long poem," saturated in Olson and Black Mountain imitation, immune to the idea it was inauthentic. I was showing Mark pieces of it at happy hour a couple of times a week, sure it was very good, that I was discovering my own "voice," as he used that confusing workshop nomenclature for the first time in my hearing to characterize the moment a poet masters language. My little allegory, however, was shit. I would like to say it was the first poem and leave it at that; that everything preceding this stylish dip into the silt bottom of the stream of consciousness was prologue; that resisting my orientation toward the spiritual, I avoided writing a sermon; that allegories of the Middle Ages had not been so obviously a major part of my early reading. To think of "the first poem" as a personal failure is to invert a certain standard. Without a standard how can anyone settle on a definition? There may be millions of definitions, yet if the term "poem" could stand for a kind of light, the best might keep it lit longest, and the worst snuff it out, making it only partly a poem, as mine was, which is to say "half alive," "still breathing," "not quite dead."

A few years later, in yet another phase of the career (another exaggeration whose definition I inflate by lack of standards), I arrived at this rather bloated definition: "Poetry is the practice of directing a line of thought illuminated by an arrangement of language of a diamond quality—rare, hard, sharp, incalculable—through a vortex of intuition built on emotion and reason and leading to clarity in human life, planetary affirmation, and priceless breath." I think it suits the expression of an ideal, and for all its romantic demands, does at least make demands of poetry. It notifies me of what I'd been working toward in those years copying the great poets. Galway Kinnell said a poet must bring his or her entire life to bear in a poem. Such a requirement defines a person as much as the act of making poems. It demands a level of concentration and risk artists and crafts people achieve at peak moments, qualifications unknown to me when I leaped from conscious imitation and studious translation into writing my own first draft of the "epic-lite," a masterpiece of lowered expectations. I suppose that advocating for standards in the early stages of writing is to argue with William Stafford's famous advice to lower one's standards in order to keep writing. Interpreting a "lowered standard" as a battle flag, however, indicates that the pacifist and conscientious objector advocated acceptance over aggressively "writing through."

Mark's encouragement was, surprise-surprise, half-hearted at best. He'd say, "Can you fit the word 'roseate' right here?" Or: "Don't juxtapose two abstractions; follow abstractions with concrete nouns, like 'mathematical peach!'" When I reached what was surely the final draft, I asked him to take it until Friday. Since I believed I had written something quite good, I anticipated Mark's perceptive reading, disposed to accept editorial advice as Eliot did Pound's. I grew impatient Friday with the ordering of beer, pretzels, fetching the glass, the pouring, salute, and a moment to stare into space. Our waitress, Andrea, was married to an actor. We found this out our first happy hour. One Friday I confessed to Mark that I was in love with her. Like the first poem, this too was exaggerated. I was too shy to say more than hello and order my beer, but in one of our sessions Mark declared to Andrea and the room that she and I were "electric together" and should have an affair. Embarrassed as I was, I liked her knowing how I felt enough that I had kept coming back, and now while I waited for Mark to say something about my manuscript, I thought his comments would impress her too.

I must have had more than one beer because my reaction was too abrupt to have been completely sober. He noted a few details, a line or two worth praise, but came quickly to the point: I should stop trying to write poetry altogether. I don't remember what I said or if I said anything, but I know I got up quickly and began to storm out of there. I must have appeared furious because he told me not to get mad; he only meant I should quit *trying*. Whether he was being conciliatory for my sake, or so that he wouldn't be left alone to drink the pitcher, Mark's dropping the other shoe only made me seethe further. I was sure he thought I was so bad I should quit, and I saw him as a pompous ass. Perhaps Olson would have told me the same, or I would have learned, had I gone, that death frees us from imitation, that poets and everyone else discover how to die from dying. That "copying

71

the great poets" may make our poems correct, but whether they are or not, our lives like our deaths become our own. I grabbed my manuscript, my pack, my scarf which I tossed over a shoulder like Shelley might have had he been told off by that doddering idiot Wordsworth, and got the hell out of there.

The first poem is a matter of setting limits. What were you satisfied with? When did you know it was right? When did you make your first work of art? One answer might be, "I've yet to write my first poem." Not that I went right on to the second, but that in calling something a poem, the ideal is beyond what we settle for. Did Dante think he achieved the perfect expression of his vision? It's hard to believe any poet can say, "This is it, this is what I had in mind, and this is just as I heard the words." If it is facile to assume that fulfillment is the reward for creating great art, how can we expect a poem to make its author happy? I was shielded from that inconvenience; my apprenticeship, which had just come to an end, consisted of imitation and translation. Searching for spiritual insights to confirm those I recognized, I risked nothing. There was nothing true in my lengthy allegorical attempt. No compassion, no sorrow, no deliberate celebration, no voice all my own. I hadn't noticed how skillfully I'd learned to imitate. I left that bar and stepped into the street where snow was falling, the old army knapsack stuffed with new used poetry books. Irate as I may have felt toward him, I realized Mark had pointed out the vein of fools' gold I'd been working. And now that he had, there was no need of him. My obsessive imitations had no purpose other than to gain form, which as the *Heart Sutra* tells us, is empty, and as Olson says on the first page of *Maximus,* "love is form, and cannot be without important substance." I could walk down the street free of mentors, in revolt from the old ways, and, without a map but unable to speak the truth; I wanted to flee my limitless capacity for mimicry. The flight of the poem forming its own wings out of fire—even out of tin—doesn't make it a phoenix, but it does illuminate. A few months later, in love for once, I wrote my first poem.

HOW I CHANGED

Faulty memory makes good memoir. It was "Wooden Ships," not "Four Dead in Ohio." My world view must have shifted prior to Kent State rather than later. It rehabilitates me: not money made me see myself a creature driven and derided by vanity, but brutality—in those deaths, close to home.

Crosby Stills Nash & Young at Boston Garden and a flashy blazer, bright yellow tie, a beautiful woman, blond bouffant, regal for front-row seats. Her ermine, her silks, her red dress, shoulders glossy under dizzying spotlights. I drove a freezer truck to Cape Cod's best restaurants, and in Boston in suits stood out front of major theaters directing folk lining a block for *Midnight Cowboy, Zabriskie Point,* and who knows what else now faded into the bye and bye, though I watched a hundred times. When I got bored, I smoked—at a distance from other assistant managers; I preferred Jean-Louis Trintignant.

I could just afford Boston Garden. I was the guy with the babe cold as luscious snow, hot as steel strings. Heads turned, jaws went slack. We were ushered to wooden seats not ten feet from the stage by a white-haired man in white gloves; we were more the show than their mellifluous voices warning of a gentle lost future which meant little they sounded so good, and I was much the shiny dude down front with a voluptuous prize, a racetrack beauty, diva of cocktail parties, the future Wife of Bath.

Then the lights dimmed, the stage ready. Someone came for a sound check, joke, or the introductions. We were in hardwood seats, yes, but in the direct shadow of the greatest singers so no problem really, the seats were worthy of extravagance. Just then "Wooden Ships . . ."—it must have been. How could I have known the events recorded in "Four Dead in Ohio" and still strut about in such clothes and blonds of vanity? The lights went out and twenty or thirty, perhaps a hundred smoky, dirty, barefoot, big-haired people rushed to sit on the floor and fill the front of the stage, the aisles, front rows, and they squatted right beside me.

Memory is conspiratorial, as was the cherubic smile of the person closest to me. A boy or a girl? Someone my age. Dressed like the others, long greasy hair—and happy—they were all so happy. My money was wasted. I turned from them to the glistening body beside me and didn't know who she was. Laughing and stretching out along the floor were the only people I ever wanted to know.

LOVE & HATE

At dawn before cars filled Harvard Square, a man outside a coffee shop bent down and rolled his pants above the calf muscle, carefully prodding the enlarged vein with a needle. It was the second day of a riot that lasted three days and nights. Some white students printed a leaflet calling on workers and students to support the struggle of blacks in the ghetto. After leafletting all day, we met at home. Ronny had his brother's car, a '63 maroon Chrysler with large fins. Since Yousef had joined the Panthers, we had less contact. Now and then a call; last time it was just, "We need guns." Ronny and Jones got some family heirlooms—a shotgun, twenty gauge, single barrel, and a .22 rifle. Bobby bought a thirty-caliber carbine; a perfect urban guerrilla gun, it had a clip. We hid them in the trunk and started over to Kenny's. We would have to go through shooting and fires, but we didn't anticipate how conspicuous our faces would be. Police blocked the shortcuts; an unmarked car swerved to a stop sideways on the expressway and a plainclothesman jumped out facing oncoming traffic with a shotgun. Some police were in buses and some with firemen. Parked cars were burning; small explosions could be heard upstairs in some of the burning buildings. I heard the sound of glass shattering everywhere, and gunshots. We were all afraid. There wasn't going to be time to say we were cool, we had guns to deliver. We felt helpless looking out of the slow Chrysler at hundreds of deranged faces. I had never seen such hatred; the frank lack of restraint, their mouths and eyes wide, made me shrink to the bottom of humility. A loud blast went off behind us as we came to the phalanx of police in helmets rushing the street and waving clubs. "There's a hole," Jones said, "Go, Go Go!" and Ronny shot down a side street. "I think they set the bank on fire," he said. We got through and there was brick dust everywhere and, sprayed on one wall, "Skinny and No Baby!" We couldn't return to the house. After passing out those leaflets, we could be arrested. Ronny dropped us at Marg's apartment. Jones and Betsy slept on the other side of the partition. We could hear him snoring. Marg and I were in her big bed. "Pretend you're riding a bicycle," she said. "Slow! Go slow, slower, slower." I exaggerated the slowness, thinking of Sundays and pebbles and smooth wheels, and passing deserted factories while a bird sang. I loved to feel her breath on my ear. "Where are you now?" she asked. "Mass Ave." Then she said, "Just keep peddling. Don't come yet." She was smiling. Stop thinking. Just peddle. But we went faster, and we got louder; she was laughing and I was laughing, too. Then Bobby's head was above us over the partition, one eye squinting that had been closed by shrapnel the year before. "It's all right! It's only a chicken bone!" I asked him what he was talking about. "It's a chicken bone . . . it's . . . oh . . . oh, I'm sorry . . . I must have . . . I must have been dreaming. I thought you had a chicken bone caught in your throat, and you were dying."

"ALL WATCHED OVER BY MACHINES OF LOVING GRACE"

My father was annoyed the first time I told him, so he acted like he didn't hear me, and asked a second time, "You walked?" My mother didn't mind, since I was home okay. She minded later. Again and again she lay awake nights imagining me "in some ditch," as she liked to put it, "with your head split open," and there's no way she would even know because the hospital wouldn't get in touch with your own mother. We were on the front porch or in the living room; why ask for the third time, feigning disbelief that I had come loping up the long avenue the length of our little peninsula? "You walked?" It was the first week of June, 1960. Seniors had been released from the local high school; finished with finals, they drove around in drunken packs in the middle of the afternoon. I didn't go to that school. In October we had moved to the South Shore, gateway to Cape Cod, thirty miles from Boston where Dad was paying tuition at a Catholic high school and not about to let me switch to public school after the agony he'd undergone preparing me to attempt, and finally fail, the entrance exam for the prestigious Jesuit school. Kind to a fault, he blamed the cold I had on the day of the exam. After drilling me with practice exams for three years, he must have been sorely disappointed, but to his credit, he only showed concern for me—and worry that I too would begin to lose confidence and hope. He helped me enter the other Catholic school whose entrance exam I'd passed earlier as practice for the Jesuits and hedge against failure. So now that I was attending second choice, we drove in every morning to Boston in quiet resignation, and he dropped me off in Dorchester where he had another ten years left at the Post Office, put me on the subway, and let me take buses home in the afternoon for a couple of hours to our new house.

Maybe I walked a mile or so that day, but after I got a ride as soon as I stuck my thumb out. My little bag, my school coat, my tie, marked me as private school coming home from downtown Boston. Months of waiting for the slow neighborhood bus in rain, snow and now early summer evening sunlight had me worn down. With more fear of Dad finding out than of dangerous drivers who might pick me up, a cute wiffle-headed kid twitching with worry, I screwed up my courage and feigned nonchalance. The car was full. All seniors, they looked like the football team; I was told don't sit in the passenger seat, get in the back, sit in the middle, and off we went. I got in of my own free will. Why? Maybe it would have been more embarrassing to say no thanks, I'll wait for the next ride. All I really remember is their rat of a car pulling away from the curb and one of them saying, "We're gonna kill ya, kid."

The next ride was similar: the driver also suggested he could kill me. Was it the years of Fifties TV paying off? Or my mother's voice which prepared me for fame—who could resist? How could I not impress the world with my upbringing? Whatever it was drivers saw in my face, my lack of skepticism saved my life, a ration of gullibility disproportionately allotted me long before I hit the streets. This guy wore a black shirt and string tie, long greasy hair tied back. He was the first person I ever met who seemed dangerous. Even when he asked what I thought kept him from plugging me with that gun in his glove box, I assumed he was simply acting responsibly and trying to scare me into taking the bus again when he offered to drive off the road and kill the two of us. After he kicked me out at the next light, gave me a grim stare and took off, I still had an unsullied faith in the good will of others. No real harm would come to me because people helped one another.

Other drivers appear in memory as indifferent, large, working-class alcoholics; some knew my parents, though I didn't see how. There was one girl, but I was further on in high school taking rides during summer break. Her boyfriend told her never pick up hitchhikers, but she didn't see anything wrong, and by the way, that's my house right there—where do you want me to drop you? She had nice legs, excellent fingernails, and didn't want to kill me.

When I entered the seminary in sophomore year, my father was pleased, and I wondered if his original plan had been to get me to become a Jesuit. Not the least cause of his delight that I wanted to spend my life celibate and poor, teaching kids he'd found unteachable twenty years earlier before heading for the mailroom in the Irish thug district of Dorchester, was that I would no longer thumb a ride home from school. Seven years later, he fetched me from the seminary, kind, not mentioning failure, I wouldn't tell him I'd discovered celibacy to be intolerable. He would never ask how I got there if I arrived on his doorstep without a car, though he often gave hitchhikers a ride. During my freshman year, we became friends with the early morning regulars who caught us before we jerked onto 3A toward Boston. We didn't threaten to kill anyone and no one offered to kill us. I would live most of my life without knowing what killing is. One night I left his house after another argument about my hair length or the war in Vietnam.

I don't know why I entered the seminary even after a clergyman molested me, though mine was not as drastic as the violations of thousands who've accused priests of sexual misconduct. Many priests have been accused of worse abuse, and I can rarely accept their innocence or that of bishops who moved them to unsuspecting parishes. Just before he died, my father and I had a little talk about the archbishop of Boston; I couldn't tell him how much I was hoping for the bankruptcy his own diocese had been worrying about in the national news, the exposure of those priests, and the downfall of that prelate who, he insisted, was a good man. The brother who did that to me should have been a warning, but I kept on anyway, having declared to him, Father Director, my parents and the world at large, that I would enter the seminary, and become a priest; threatening drivers should have been warning enough to make me a lifetime advocate of public transportation. But neither warning took. I stayed in that seminary till just after Woodstock, which may have been in part responsible for my urge to hit the road.

The Newport Jazz Festival Riot, as the 1968 Festival came to be known, was more extravagant than its organizers anticipated because of the many people from New England and around the country who hadn't bought a ticket and were locked out. It wasn't Woodstock. A chain-link fence and security guards encircled the event's old wood fence, which blocked the view from a nearby hill, full of dancers and picnickers tripping on LSD and getting louder and more boisterous as night descended. By dark the crowd formed a wedge against a weak point in the fence and began pushing in a friendly manner, all in good fun. Inside the fence the guard didn't think so, and threatened, sending off scratchy messages on his walky-talky while yelling at everybody. When all that weight was about to crash the wire fence down on him, he ran away, and hundreds fell over one another trampling both fences, the screech of nails separating from planks. The music became suddenly loud as the crowd entered on cue; though jazz patrons sat comfortably in a fabricated grove upon a real meadow, the triumphant voice of Dionne Warwick sang for us, sang of liberation, sang happily, giddy, that familiar welcoming refrain—"Do You Know The Way To San Jose?"

It didn't take long for tear gas, riot gear, marching us out through official escort in an orderly line down the road to be processed and sent into the night. Before being quelled, though, the first squad of rebels took the stage, seized the mike from a gentle gray-haired man in a clean suit, all but in tears with the strain of trying to get things back in order, pleading with us to go back beyond the perimeter. Dionne was whisked off stage. He gave up the mike to a person I had seen earlier while wandering among campsites. I'd stumbled up to a fire, and was passed a bottle and a joint, and listened as the man now telling us "we have liberated this stage," negotiated with two brother bikers the cost for one of his three girlfriends.

When I slipped away from that campfire, many people along a path were out looking for connections, joking, displaying hair and makeup as anti-style. A man in a white T-shirt and thin black hat, holding a large garbage bag, called out to passersby: "I want a friend! Somebody be my friend tonight! I've got forty-five hits of acid for a friend!" I came upon a crowd in an open field, swaying, arms draped over shoulders, waving bottles, a synchronized kick. They were looking up at a tower, shouting at the top of their lungs: "JUMP! JUMP!"On the fourth story of the concrete tower stood a young man, chest painted in bright neon, teetering unsafely over the parapet.

That was all before the concert had begun, before we laid our blankets casually down on the grassy hillside to listen as if shepherds and poets of the pastoral tradition around the walls of Rome to haunting melodies inside—Dionne, and Ray, Miles, and Buddy, Sonny, and one trio after another till you couldn't take it anymore, and they finally shooed you away, because of the mess with the fences, on down the road into the night where I for one managed to scramble to a beach and watch the tide until dawn, when I caught a ride with a grim biker who never said a word as he pulled up beside me, barefoot and wrapped in my faded blanket, shuffling back to the remains of our tear-gassed campsite.

In my notebook was scribbled the one idea I took away from the festival: "I need to travel." When I got home and recovered, it was summer and I went to California. Why? Because everybody did; it wasn't an original destination, but I wanted to see Haight-Ashbury, though it was almost too late to know what happened below the detritus of head shops, leather shops, cafes and boutiques. I couldn't just go clean; I had to take along a beautiful German shepherd named Rachel. My father tried to convince me the dog was a mistake, no longer trying to get me to stay. The last thing he said was my grandmother told him not to worry about the beard and long hair; I'd grow out of it.

The fact was, I didn't like the dog, and the dog didn't care for the trip or me; I gave her to a girl in Madison, Wisconsin, at a benefit for a draft resister. I remember walking her through Montreal and Quebec City, where Quebecois Separatists took me in and my meager French came in handy. A car picked us up beyond Ontario, and the couple up front seemed increasingly more foreign the closer we got to Detroit. The woman was young, but not the driver's daughter. He was a professor of economics, or law, or philosophy and maybe she was his student. It hadn't entered my consciousness that such a person could be married to this stiff in the driver's seat. She spoke about him as if she were his representative to the Press. "Ralph believes in having answers. He likes what you are doing. Here, Ralph wanted you to have this," and she handed me ten dollars American as I got out; back on native soil, I was holding my pack and Rachel's leash, while their gray Caddy paddled away from the curb.

A ride from Knoxville to Albuquerque became a tribal event as a big white Plymouth toted six or seven of us, but for the first day it was just Michael, the driver, and me. After he kept me waiting an hour outside a bar in Memphis, he apologized, and off we went. The longest conversation we had involved songs on the radio. He had a lot to say, but I can't recall about what. We picked up the next hitchhiker, and Michael was rattling off a fragment of his life story, as we heard "Candy Man," by Sammy Davis Junior. "That's me!" he said. I didn't understand until he sped up to a VW microbus painted psychedelic toadstool, and told me roll down that window, they want to buy acid. "What?" "Roll it down!" He was driving erratically, shouting and motioning them to pull over. We stopped, he sold the drugs, and off we went. It went like this for quite some time, though not through the Panhandle of Texas. As we entered New Mexico, a roadblock stopped us. We were about four people in the back seat—a guy carrying a long bow on his way to Denver, and two very cute girls with lilting southern accents from Chatahoochee. Some big men up front grumbled about gas stations and bank robberies. Finally the police got to our long white car. Registration? Not his car. Driver's license? Not his. In the trunk, twenty-five guns of varied caliber, ammunition, and three hundred hits of LSD. The roadblock was for him, the car stolen. They let the rest of us go. The guy with the bow and the two girls disappeared in the big rocks beside the freeway.

I reached San Francisco on a freight train I'd hopped in Denver. Barefoot on railroad ballast, I picked up a pair of too small tennis shoes at the Salt Lake Free Store. A hobo pulled out a knife and sliced the toes so I could wear them like sandals. The coal car dropped me in Oakland outside a diner, which I entered with a small Mexican man who didn't expect anything but a cup of coffee. I offered him breakfast, and we went in as proud citizens. Surprised, the waitress gave me the same look she gave him, and treated me as rudely; I thought I'd better wash my hands. My face in the mirror was black with coal dust.

By October one crisp dawn I was staring into hundreds of spider webs, their architecture spread through Scotch Broom and weighted with hefty drops of dew, no spiders, nothing dangling in the cupboard; I heard a chord formed on the coastal air by two antique motors of twin Ford pickups rolling in tandem downhill to the intersection toward which I'd slowly moped facing a bleak first light with my thumb out. Dropped the night before in a quiet burg on Highway One where dawn was a rumor, I watched the first pickup pull over. Nobody stopped for hitchhikers before ten as a rule, though my experience then was only limited to southern states, the Southwest, the east coast, and northeastern Canada. The other pickup pulled over behind him. As I hoisted my gear into the first, I heard someone call my name. Two guys the night before gave me a wool sweater and a pair of shoes, and hugged me as if we'd been life-long buddies when they drove home to their warm cabins. I'd met a young couple and camped with them on the beach two nights earlier. The woman thought I had some guru-like insight into relationships, and kept whispering about the one she was having with our driver every time he got out to pay for gas or ask directions. I didn't expect to see any of them again.

A woman opened the passenger door of the other pickup, and I struggled with a seizure of magical thinking—the universe indeed was my old neighborhood in Dorchester where friends appeared unexpectedly and no one noticed wrinkles in the space-time continuum. Here was Susie Goldwitz, whom I'd last seen in Boston six months ago; we were two dots approaching one another on the giant screen tracking everyone's movements, yet we had known one another well, as real people, not long ago. She was heading to Victoria, and of course fully intended to hitchhike all the way alone, as she had across the country.

A few years later in British Columbia, Rick Wood and I were escorted out of a rail yard. We thought it would be easy to hop freight trains in Canada and travel to Boston. I hadn't seen my family for several years by then, and Rick needed to get away from a potentially hot scene in Seattle. We were so wrong about the freight yards. Unlike American yards, men in suits scrutinized what went on around the trains in Vancouver. Here no one pointed out our train to us as American rail workers did. No one told us to hide from the yard bull. Ticketed and ejected from the yard within fifteen minutes, we decided to hitchhike across the Canadian inter-provincial highway system.

Two days later and fifty miles east, angry and tired, we stood across the highway from each other hitchhiking in opposite directions. But nobody came, so we forgot about being mad, started talking again and walked ten miles until a car finally stopped. Eventually we crossed the border. Not without incident. I was searched and held until a call from Alaska confirmed I wasn't the guy they were looking for on a murder charge. A group of survivalists gave us an ominous ride. A drunk rolled our car into the center island. A young girl wrecked the company car she was transporting across Montana right in front of us. We were five men, the driver asleep in the back seat; no one spoke to the pretty girl—pouting out the window and tough as nails—while we shuttled her from the accident to her boss in Bozeman. I had to go to an emergency room, convinced I was having a heart attack—chest pains for a thousand miles. Just stress, said the doctor, heart attacks are on the other side.

The longest loop, a freight train from Denver, was on a flat car where we found comfortable places below a semi rattling behind forty-three others to the Windy City. The ride was only one night, but started with a bad omen when two children pointed real guns at me. We were out where everybody could see us, and it hadn't gotten dark; the train easing across neighborhood intersections gave ample opportunity to line up my melon between their little sight hairs. Two years after *Easy Rider* I wouldn't have stood out in a crowd of extras; like many on the road, I made a good target for those lamenting on bumper stickers: "The things you see when you don't have a gun." Once, outside a Mexican village in southern Colorado, someone made a fire near the road; the same cars all night circling, film noir music where someone might go crazy any moment, my mother's greatest fear come true. At the outskirts of a New Mexico town, my last ride would be back in an hour and pick me up if I was still there. Be careful, he said, last week they shot an archeologist in the desert. Right there, that's where they shot him, as they drove by. I have spent only one more terrible and frightening hour on the road, but I was the driver. No one else stopped, my ride returned, took me a hundred miles east; but not before three trucks passed ten times, shotguns mounted in rear windows. I couldn't have been more shootable dressed in a clown suit.

On the trains we hadn't expected to be vulnerable. We thought our train would stop and we could run to a freight car

85

and climb in. There we would be inside and safe, unless the car was occupied, in which case we'd have to worry about those old 'bo's protecting territory and getting a good night's sleep without a bunch of *whining hippies squawkin' and drinkin' that electric wine those kids drink—where'd you get that shit, anyway? What's got you kids so fucked up?* In any case the train didn't stop. It sailed at eighty miles an hour to Chicago. During the night, I woke up startled on the edge of the flat car; the noise unbearable, I was afraid I would roll off and die in the wilderness, or go crazy from rumbling and clanging, and throw myself off. I was desperate enough to see the world had narrowed to two choices: die by accident or intent. Rick was my one hope, and I worried for an hour before crawling to where he lay against a dusty backpack to ask him to hold me, and keep me from jumping. The experience didn't affect him the same way; maybe his conscience is clean, I thought. On mine was the blame for everything—the disaster of this trip I talked him into, cares and loves and hates abandoned on both coasts, my wasting life, my father's disappointment, my sorry self, I thought, as we ripped along in the shelter of a semi shaking so violently side to side it could tear itself loose and derail the train.

By daylight we rolled and squeaked into Chicago, the transfer point for durable goods to the Midwest, hundreds of acres of track covered by trains. The yard was roaring with braking and banging cars as we rolled through shouts of yard workers and engineers. Our flat car was among others full of hogs and poultry when we hopped off. One of the crew said our train would have taken us across the yard to catch out to Boston. "Here," he said, "jump into that caboose while it's going slow. Stay down low while you're in there, and don't let the flatfoot see you guys." "Flatfoot?" "You know, the gumshoe." "What?" He was speaking another language, from detective novels I didn't recognize in this context. I would have said the yard bull. I think he finally tried "the train dick" and I understood. "The Black Panthers hijacked a car loaded with guns last week, and they

86

been shooting at trains from them boarded-up buildings, so keep low."

We hoisted ourselves into the caboose just as it left that section of yard and found a place on the floor behind a cabinet. The train moved gracefully for miles out of the yard and through a tunnel. Under a freeway I could see brick buildings and boards on the windows. While I was peering out an alarm went off, and we cringed into the corner farthest from the entrance. Moments later the door opened, and we saw the head and shoulders of a man in a brown suit and tie. We ducked down, but he'd already seen us, and he was taking out his pistol.

Before we got to the end of that track, we counted every dollar and figured we could afford two bus tickets. What could happen on a bus? Nothing, really nothing happened. We didn't sleep. Some babies cried. A girl and boy made out for a few hundred miles. Then the bus dropped us off early in the morning near some complicated rotary in southern New England. It turned out we didn't have enough to get all the way to Boston. It was already humid, and air-conditioned commuters were on their way to work. Wearing suits, clean, well-fed, with deodorant and aftershave, light cotton shirts and ties, they drove compact vehicles with radio stations I'd been unable to listen to since the drug dealer got arrested. A morning filled with light and the hazy dew of June, our spot in the center of an island gave us hitchhiking privileges in all directions. Crisscrossing the island and the overpass, and looping in from every side were the power lines of New England, slack between the most magnificent towers I had ever seen. We were far from our own town, but I was home, from whence the ugly and deteriorated century of industry had come, and the invasion of every space, the occupation of air, the ground, magnetic forces of consciousness, and even the invasion of the will.

We knew we would be there a long time. No one was going to stop, and we would have to wait for travelers who had passed the night alone and wanted to talk. No one for a long time had offered to kill me in so many words. No one was trying to scare me. Instead they wore me down with talk, bored me to death, which was eventually why I quit hitchhiking.

Those power lines dangling between monstrous towers impressed me beyond description. They symbolized my home. It would be good to see my mother and sisters, and old friends, but I was reluctant to think about my father after all these years. We stopped talking, or I stopped phoning. He could not have gotten in touch with me except by mail, which he did several times. But I hadn't written back. I wanted to fix things, and finally say, "I love you, Dad," and know he was proud of me. Of course, it wasn't going to work that way. We had our visit, and my appearance threw him off—something about the clothes, the hair again, the beard, something I said about the war. I was exempt from the draft, lucky in the lottery; he didn't want me to go anyway. He'd flown thirty missions over Japan, the first during Tokyo's horrific firebombing when his B-29 took flak in the bomb-bay doors, the Distinguished Flying Cross dusty in a drawer upstairs he never once mentioned. I found it only after his death. We had our quick visit, a sandwich in a café, and I looked for some floor space with friends in Cambridge.

Rick and I stayed the rest of that week, and one night while we were at a party, the radio announced Nixon's resignation. Out of touch with the news while we had crossed the country, we'd forgotten that Watergate and the impeachment proceedings occupied the American mind; men sound asleep in front of televisions came alert the moment a wife or child turned down the volume on the hearings and commentary. After the announcement the entire party moved into Harvard Square, teeming with people drunk on champagne, throwing flags into the air. No riot police were on the streets. The crowd was peaceful, not a protest parade, but a party over the downfall of an icon. As I write this, calls for the impeachment of George W. Bush are again in the air. They began when even by optimistic estimates there were five weeks till war, judging by the moon over the Iraqi desert and the onset of a brutal summer for American soldiers, a summer which would guarantee the increase of American dead, and the weakening of the public will. They continued when it was said the President had lied to Congress. History was hardly repeating itself, though calling for a leader to step down predates the Bible. A rational person in the context of Vietnam was a "dove," and today letters to the editor in my local paper ridicule neighbors and friends who stand along the overpasses of the freeway that runs through our town and wave anti-war signs. Those letters don't use the avian terminology, but they see only one possibility for a patriot. I hear my father's voice though he too opposed Bush's policies; it's the voice I was afraid to go home to that morning in June, yet looked forward to hearing. An America historically split between the intolerant and tolerant buzzed those power lines strung on infinite identical towers.

In my years of travel, America had been generous. The road never let me doubt I'd get a ride eventually, and always arrive safe at my destinations. I lived in this cloud, protected as if by gods. Who didn't know he was indestructible? We trust in our history of good health and escapes from near-death. I went a long time not knowing tragedy and assumed life was not serious. I had never witnessed an accident of any kind, had never seen anyone die. Yet my life seemed like a series of ironies when I struck and killed an 82-year-old woman crossing the highway from her mailbox, her fliers and junk mail sprayed over the road. Condolences from friends and acquaintances puzzled both them and me. We don't know what to say, we are so sorry. "I can't imagine what that feels like." I tell them I hope they never know. I don't tell them about the terror and disbelief and physical revulsion. She died of a head injury, her death instantaneous. I could not block out any encounter with police, medics, family, neighbors, and passers-by. I witnessed their grief and their confusion, and the end of my life-long illusion. Everything my father always knew was true: death is a moment away.

Nixon was peering through the curtains of the White House when Americans suspected a similar insecurity about the goodness of their cause, when the media helped inure us to bodies in ditches, lists of dead young soldiers, and outrage in the screams of Vietnamese children. Rick and I were stranded in traffic aware only of morning light. We told whatever lyrics, jokes, or stories we had memorized. The power lines reminded me of Richard Brautigan's poem, "All Watched Over by Machines of Loving Grace," which takes the pervasion of devices further than my own epiphany. It would be hours before the Hell's Angel in a restored Chevy from California gave us a lift for nearly the last leg of the journey. He was on his way to repay a debt just south of Boston. A woman he cared for had terrible scars across her face from a board with a spike wielded by the man he was on his way to see. I would remember him as we entered Boston in a priest's car, the radio blaring Simon and Garfunkel's "All Gone to Look for America," arguing above their beautiful voices with the priest about reason and faith, power and forgiveness, deluding myself that hatred was philosophical, not personal.

Another irony, the residue of anger I fed most of those years as a passenger joined my own fondness for the dim notes and phrases I sang from Gregorian chant. Before we left our island, when we ran out of stories and poems, I began to recite the Latin Mass. Rick and the passing drivers were my parish, and that hazy hill with power lines my altar. *"Introibo ad altare Dei,"* I began, remembering the opening of Joyce's *Ulysses*, words at the service of my pagan worship of the dawn, of my native land, of friendship, as if I could trust not the plan of the universe, or a force guiding my life, but only the accident that brought me here.

A LETTER TO DAN PETERS

It was busier than usual here the day your book arrived; my mailbox was full, and so were the phone messages. A book from the poet Bill Yake, yours, plus the usual ream of crap in the mail. Good news on the phone, too. After a year-long fight with AT&T, they're calling off the dogs, admitting that fourteen hundred dollars worth of roaming fees was as I told them due to a stolen phone and not me, the criminal genius, the little guy, the untrustworthy customer. Hurray for the unincorporated world! But I couldn't get to any of this, or answer messages, even got in trouble with my wife because I didn't pick up the phone. I had to read every word of your book as soon as I came in the door.

You don't spend a lot of time describing the accident, but I recognize its ripple through your life. That's been true for me. My one-year anniversary made me fearful, not sure why. I drove the road for the first time in months, and haven't since. A detail that struck me was you at eighteen sitting down pulling grass. I've imagined this scene over and over—you, the grass, your hair, fingers, people not talking, bright sun, the terror a teenager must feel, wondering if it's what I felt. My reaction was to stand in the middle of the scene and try to find out as much as possible. I am reminded of my father taking my son and me, my two sisters, and nieces to a simple breakfast and a visit for an hour or so. He kept standing in the middle of the fast food joint asking people to hurry and get us our order. And asking each of us: "Did you get your orange juice? Do you have the donut you wanted?" It annoyed me he couldn't let people behave as they're supposed to. He finally sat, too distraught to enjoy the minutes we had.

91

I was standing like that, mouth open, asking everybody what happened, telling those who asked I didn't know how she got in front of my truck on a fifty-mile-an-hour highway. My neighbor saw me and pulled over after the emergency vehicles and troopers arrived. As she approached, I said, "I think I killed someone." She offered to call my wife on her phone, but we were so far in the sticks nobody's cell phones worked. Before her relatives came running, I could not bend down to where she was, could not step across the ditch where she'd been thrown, or look anywhere but at her, or talk to her, her back to me, gray hair with twigs. I could not believe she was not going to move. I didn't hear her moan. I started shouting.

For those minutes my terror was so great I was certain she would stand up, get better, could not possibly be dead. These things didn't happen to me; I was not that person. My sense of unreality fought against the desire to ask if she was alive. When the people came out of her house, one was the older man I had admired weeks before sitting on his tractor in their field, one of my favorite meadows. He called her name with increasing alarm, and then something about the way he said her name made me guess he wasn't surprised, that he had thought someday she would be killed returning from the mailbox; that's what I wanted to think. Her niece held her, covered her up, and kept talking to her. I resisted asking if she was dead. A young man out from the nearby farm began to berate me: "I don't see how . . . " but stopped, recognizing the futility now of blame.

Eventually a woman with the EMT told me she'd died instantly; they were taking her to Emergency where they would tell the family. They insisted on leaving hope, but told me outright. All that afternoon, through interrogations with troopers, the accident report, a talk with a pastor, no one accused me. She was in the middle of the road where she shouldn't have been; it was a tragedy. How did I not see her? I don't know, I told them many times. I loved driving through that little valley, the eastern slope of the Cultus range on one side, Cascade foothills on the other. Why didn't I notice a thin, gray-haired woman walking from her mailbox until I was fifteen feet away? I stood on the brake with my full weight, unable to turn out of the lane and avoid her. All my life I have been the driver who just misses the deer or rabbit, even the child. When I got out of my truck in the middle of the road, I couldn't help her get back up, or pick up her mail spread over the asphalt.

My wife made arrangements for me to see a counselor. The counseling appointments were vital, and continued a few weeks until I was out of the prolonged shock the counselor diagnosed. Then I gave it up. Helpful as the woman was, it was hard to get a word in edgewise. I never found someone else. Maybe my recovery—you used the word in a way I hadn't ever thought applied to me, Dan—got stalled somewhere in there. Although I've done all the other right things and kept my eye on my mental health all year long, I still feel, an insight prompted by your book, as though I am one of the wounded. I can't re-enter life serene and content.

I appreciate your willingness to show that in a poem. I can't help thinking that even with your compassionate eye toward students, you never fully let go of the boy who died. It is a kinship I feel reading your poetry, unluckily for us, a sad brotherhood. The counselor told me people would come forward to tell about accidents; you're the first. I'm grateful you let me know how we survive, and yet how we won't get over it.

My father never got over his participation in the deaths of Japanese citizens during bombing missions. Right out of the military, he hired on with the Post Office, got up and did it every day. Never complained, even when he worked a second job. Other things came out when he was drinking. Many times he had to be manager of the Post Office with a hangover. My mother used to send me to the corner saloon, where I sat on the stoop below swinging doors, until some uniformed guy asked Frank Daley to come to supper. One night my mother, my sister and I huddled in the bed, door open to the kitchen where he

93

was throwing dishes, pots and pans; the long kitchen knife twanged in the floor, linoleum turned up at its edges. Years later he was throwing dinner plates around the room during the actual dinner. He never hit my mother or any of us. Returning sergeants like my Dad were supposed to suck it up, work all day, have a few stiff belts before and after dinner, fight or fuck the wife, and sleep it off. He was pretty much delayed, and not recovering the rest of his life. Meaner and meaner those last years, he must have been in a lot of pain. His sour advice over the phone every couple of weeks, "Never get old, Pal. Shoot yourself first!" repeated to me, his only son and heir. On his deathbed four months ago, spoon fed orange juice thick enough to get down without choking—he'd lost the ability to swallow—he asked the nurse almost childishly, "Should I excuse myself if I have to spit up?" We composed a letter to his doctor, also a military man, but he couldn't remember whether captain or major, and this kept us from sending the letter requesting a full examination of his entire body because he thought there was something wrong. We completed a two-sentence letter to the doctor and he was very proud. Showed it to his orange-juice nurse: "This is very good," she said. "*I* thought so." He died the next day.

In his last hours, all that was left of him was the squint with which he approached any problem. Bushy eyebrows knit together on each inhale; exhales took sometimes a full minute or more. My sister left me alone with him even though, as far as I knew, he couldn't hear me, but all I could do was cry like never before, and tell him I couldn't live on my own. For many years, I'd talked things over with him in our weekly phone calls. That is, I would run things by him or ask advice. Less and less the last several years. I didn't tell him about the accident. I knew he'd worry, whether out of sympathy for how I felt—which I thought unlikely—or concern I might be arrested. I didn't tell him and yet I wanted to know what he would have thought about the call I received six months after the newspaper carried a picture that didn't look like the woman whose face I'd seen in profile for a second, who had never seen me, nor heard my truck. After I read her obituary five times, a lengthy one showing she was well-loved and would be sorely missed, I was grateful to learn she had no children and was survived by cousins, nieces, and nephews. From hers I learned to write a suitable obituary for my father. I was struck to learn she was a member of our local Land Trust, active for many years. I made a donation in her name. The newsletter never printed the dedication from me, so her family never knew. I sent them a short letter of condolence, and, of course, did not attend the funeral. The family never contacted me as my counselor had optimistically predicted. Six months after the accident, a trooper interviewed me over the phone, to tie up details. I was shaken back to severe depression when I hung up; after all this time I had thought that, even without a final report, I could adjust to and live with the memory. Although he spoke in a kindly way, he was determined to arraign me for vehicular homicide. I wasn't as upset about a trial as about the possibility I had been driving negligently. I went out to the scene of the accident and drove the road again. Now every morning as I drive to work, I wonder if it was my fault. Another trooper said, "She's dead, you're the victim," a common formula to get drivers to fill out the report or admit guilt, yet for all his cynicism, I'm consoled by it. If I'm a victim, it's of nothing but fate or misfortune.

What if you or I had remained at school, Dan, to correct one more student essay, or speak with a teacher just one minute more? She'd have crossed the street in safety, perhaps felt the breeze as I passed behind her. I've asked myself why I didn't take longer. Is there only one possibility for our deaths? Or do we miss so many until the law of averages catches up? The trooper did not believe in accidents, only causes and effects. An acknowledgment of fate would mean I was always to be the instrument of her death or accident, that ours was not a random encounter like wind tossing branches into the street. The notion

95

of cause and effect must include your need and my need to be somewhere else, our pressure to move with the clock from one occupation to another, too busy to pull over and admire the way tall grass swayed in her pasture.

When I left the room where my father died, he was Everyman. The pinch in his eyebrows gone, mouth open, empty, cheeks hollow, his skin yellow, white hair all but gone though he'd had a haircut and shave that afternoon, . We closed his eyes, his head on the pillow; he'd been facing the ceiling all those hours slowly finding his last breath. He was no longer there, his body a husk.

Immediately after the accident the vet told me our cat had a rare inoperable cancer in his nasal passage. I decided on chemotherapy and forced pills into him; though I kept thinking I should be taking more care of myself than this cat, it was for my son. Many nights he had to face the death of his pet and couldn't comprehend its irrationality, how undeserving of death the cat was. He knew nothing of the accident I'd been in. We never talked about it. All I could do was console him over his pending loss. In the middle of the night when I could see nothing but the torments of an unforgiven life, the cat would have trouble breathing or my son would awaken in tears. Not until the first anniversary passed, and after my father died, did I find I could be of use intentionally instead of as a simple shuffling figure of duty and routine.

By the second or third dream I had a sense of relief. He pulled up outside a hospital; I was in the bed there. He was driving a '57 Chevy, green and white. In a small, loose, happy crowd of people storming the building, he walked buoyantly across the bright snow field to get to my room. The woman I'd only seen in profile in knit sweater fluttering past, headed toward another room. He wore an odd hat with earflaps, like the one in a news photo when he graduated from gunnery school in 1942, coming into the room from sunshine with the widest smile I had ever seen. The smile he used to have when I was a kid, one I hadn't seen in so long, though eleven years of cancer made his humor the more sardonic—a beatific smile, lips stretched, and cheeks swollen with happiness. I woke up like that, my face straining to smile.

III

It is bright midnight.
Heat is against the backs of our necks
as we run. Many are burning
on the road behind us.
A great light from the sky
crushed the house, the city fell down.
We were naked people running,
blackened as barbecue, shreds
whipping behind ourselves.
Our hair burnt, faces swollen,
lips ripped from the teeth.
I could not tell men from women.
The sex organs were burnt off.
My own body was uninjured
and I was in another world.
In the fragmented light
across a footbridge, two horses, dead.
I touched one, it was still warm.
Then I became afraid, I almost stepped
on a woman sitting down, her hands
searching for nipples in her blouse.
I tried to help her, taking her arm,
and all the skin came off.
She had broken legs. I'll carry you,
I said, but a thousand people
were pushing and she was lost.
For months every day I saw them die.
The gums bleed, hair falls out,
then purple spots like snake bites

along the skin. My sister, her mouth
closing around a small cake of coal.
And my husband who had never
been to the dentist. A set of teeth
in perfect condition.
They could have been his.
I buried the teeth in his grave.

HIBAKUSHA

I never went to Vietnam. I didn't desert or ask favors. My number in the draft board lottery was ridiculously high. So high in fact when it came on the TV that night while most of the country watched, I began to laugh. Maybe not a real laugh. It's hard not to exaggerate. A grin maybe, at one of the twelve junkies sunk into chairs with stuffing popped out; half of them knew what was on, two or three knew it was important to someone. The others didn't. I grinned, or laughed, to myself; too afraid of needles to have sidestepped the draft that way, my fate would be to miss the war. When I came out of the seminary, Woodstock was over. I didn't ask how to justify not going. I was afraid and didn't want to go, yet I guessed I would, and learn from the Army something I missed about discipline in the Catholic Church. I didn't want a new vow when I was starting to think for the first time all on my own, to make life up as I went along. That's why I was smiling. Fate or God weighted on scales teetering good and evil, and then let Luck have us. 343. My perfect number. It saved my ass. Yet the loneliness of the 1-A's I knew getting up the nerve to jump to Canada, the caginess of lifetime students, who plead clinically insane or gay (just tell, *tell*), were better than the nightly procession of body bags and the list with every newscast of names of the dead. My knees lurched and I nearly vomited once picturing myself in combat. The war would have been over if everyone saw his body on fire. So I didn't go to Vietnam. I'd never heard of Cambodia. I attended protests, but eventually I got tired of not being passionate. None of us were going; our lives, our children, our villages weren't the targets. We were safe, yelling in the faces of people more insulated and ineffectual than we were to stop the killing. At every protest, new friendships, love, sex. We passed out drugs sometimes and drank to oblivion and chanted silly things when silence or shrieking seemed better. I was embarrassed by the emotion. We didn't deserve love yet. I couldn't express anything myself, not in public. Asleep, your voice becomes paralyzed; you swing at the enemy but don't connect; your fists go soft; the gun won't work; the knife never strikes.

When I was about nine, on long summer afternoons I sneaked off with *Life's Pictorial World War II*. Something drew me to it. There were beautiful scenes in that book. The way sunlight ran along the side of a bomber just before takeoff in a primitive airfield in Saipan, the painted cartoon of a black and yellow smiling bumblebee. I was carried away to those jungles. And then the bodies. I turned pages of rubble and carnage. So confused were the piles that finally when I reached the photo with one body stretched gracefully in the dirt, hands as if poised for dancing, neck bloodied, shirt open, a baby with a big head rocking back and forth in the sunlit dust screaming, I would close the book for a while. I'd been present in a bad dream. Later I opened it to the section titled "Hiroshima." On a newspaper clipping tucked in there my father alongside other men was given an award for missions over Japan. An aerial photograph of a large city, burning, falling buildings. Then the bodies again, the mushroom cloud, fireball at its core. Very often I would close the book here, perhaps I was getting tired. But sometimes I enjoyed lurking. A woman stood beside a building's rubble. Bodies had been brought out of the ruin and placed without ceremony before her. Her right hand open in the air, she was crying, her mouth uncontrollably wide. Dirt and sweat gave her flesh the quality of sculpture against the blue sky. Here I always stopped, no matter my temptation to read further. I might re-read the news clip, note my father's uniform, fold the paper and put it at random into the book. No one else looked, no one knew I did. It was my own, a time and place I didn't understand, where everyone was starving. Recalling it now, I don't remember any special feeling. I must have stared hard because the faces are still familiar.

I didn't go to Vietnam. My father paid that debt. I saw the faces from that book in those who came back. Although I tried to talk about anything else, to talk around it, I wanted to know what it would have been like for me. I wanted the same hollow at the end of a sentence and not call it despair, or loneliness I wanted what they and my father had gotten from war: I wanted my life justified too. But I could never know what they saw. Faces from that war were tattooed on their eyes; when they came, like me, to a noisy bar in a small waterfront town to watch an ordinary girl pour a glass of beer and lick foam from her lip.

WITNESS

A grumble of helicopters in the early gray hours awakened Oak Bay; the Navy was in the sky, and the Coast Guard, and Channel Four, whirring blades over the sand. Everyone was moving quickly: motorized Zodiac boats were taking some out to the *Pacific Peacemaker*, others in ponchos and barefoot or in rubber boots dragged canoes and skiffs over the slick green rocks. The tide just turning, a rowing dory loaded four local careful newsmen from a tottering fiberglass skiff. We distributed our weight in a dinghy and rowed toward the *Lorraine*, a lovely twenty-foot sailboat, aboard which we would motor from Oak Bay to just within the "legal zone" near Olele Point to observe the *U.S.S Ohio*, the first Trident nuclear submarine, as it entered Puget Sound, and the acts of civil disobedience to be performed by those aboard Australia's *Pacific Peacemaker*, the *Lizard of Woz*, the *Ploughshares*, and a dozen or so two-person blockade boats. As the *Lorraine* picked up speed, four small helicopters and two "Huey's" tore overhead, followed by sleek media choppers and one or two single-engine planes. Several small motorboats headed into the legal zone.

It was 1982, and certainly a small group compared to the millions protesting America's invasions of Afghanistan and the occupation of Iraq. Though we might float home in awe when we spot a nuclear submarine today in our bays and fjords, we are not at all surprised that Puget Sound and the Hood Canal make significant targets since the Trident system made Bangor, Washington, its home base. Yet that morning our firm belief was that the arrival of the most expensive first-strike weapon ever created heralded a frightening phase of the Cold War to which we'd all grown uncomfortably accustomed. Now that the United

States has engaged in preemptive attacks, the relevance of those few protest boats seems all the more like poignant visionary warnings from a hapless Cassandra.

At Oak Bay word spread that the Coast Guard had boarded *Lizard* and power-hosed its crew inside the legal zone. The crew offered loaves of bread, holding the bread out, as civil disobedience boats did later—"Bread Not Bombs." The Coast Guard power-hosed them to set precedent and warn them off. A delivery truck driver for Indian Island Naval Base said the commander spread rumors that dynamite packets were left at the gate, and told his men their lives were in danger.

From the bow of the *Lorraine*, the water a calm gray, we saw sails far off, the mast of the *Peacemaker* from Australia, and on her sail were painted a thousand multi-colored faces. Within the restricted zone, a line of floats from Olele Point to Foulweather Bluff, many boats were shrouded in morning fog. A Coast Guard cruiser broke away from a line of strobe lights and headed toward the *Pacific Peacemaker* and two cabin cruisers. One, we thought, carried Seattle's Archbishop Hunthausen, the other was the Press. Hunthausen had announced he'd be honored if demonstrators who were arrested used him as a reference to the bail bondsman. For this and his support of sanctuary for political refugees, he'd been disciplined by "the Vatican's pit-bull," later elected Pope Benedict XVI. We spotted the medical boat, then another press boat, perhaps CBS. We later learned Hunthausen was in Spokane.

What was I doing with these peaceniks? I was the son of a warrior. My father's military career informed his entire life and my own. On these boats was a large contingent of anti-military fanatics. Not my first protest, I had marched against Vietnam ten years earlier and protested at the gates of the Trident's base in Bangor. I never talked about such activities with my father, and had no idea what his opinion of nuclear proliferation was. All I knew was that when I was a child he told me he won the war, and that he was joking; he referred to himself

105

even shortly before his death as a hero, in a style all his own, as if mocking our world's hunger for heroes.

I wasn't a military brat, but could have been. Once or twice my mother tried to convince him to re-enlist in the Air Force full time instead of taking us to New Hampshire summers while he attended the Reserves Training at nearby Grenier Airbase. She told him we wanted to travel and I wanted to attend schools all over the country, all over the world even. "But you'd have to leave your friends, and your education might suffer." I had to think about that a second, but my mother didn't think it would be a problem. In the end, he decided to quit the Reserves and work to retirement in the Post Office in our old neighborhood, commuting two hours both ways.

Some of those in protest boats who had been Army brats—or Air Force, Navy, even kids of Marines—went out on the water to find their fathers. Or perhaps most had resolved personal issues, and their pacifism had no such petty origin. Still, for me whose retired father was watching the then-hopeless Boston Red Sox from his favorite chair, the front line of protest was too far to go. Something held me back from crossing the restricted zone and seeking out the power hose, or precipitating my own arrest for civil disobedience. A simple lack of courage? Or had I from an early age come to trust the goodness of my country, and believe our military and political leaders had the best intentions? I had become incapable of listening even to the voice in my head debase the government as a murderous bunch of thugs. What brought me there was a desire to record that a gray Navy cutter and five Coast Guard boats overtook the *Peacemaker* as it motored slowly with orange civil-disobedience boats in tow, two people in wetsuits aboard each. A little to the north in our line of vision was Foulweather Bluff. The dark vague submarine form emerged from fog, a few Coast Guard boats escorting it. From this distance white walls of foam appeared to mount the sides of *U.S.S. Ohio.* Much less remarkable than expected, a story spread, later proved false, that there were two subs, and the one we'd spotted was only a Poseidon. The Coast Guard surrounded the *Peacemaker* and the cabin cruiser used by the Press. The *Peacemaker* began evasive tactics as planned, veering away from the cutter, *Point Glass*. One Coast Guard Zodiac cut the tow-line from the *Peacemaker* to the plywood civil-disobedience boats. Much later John Schell showed me a souvenir: a length of frayed and unraveled yellow line from a CD boat. I had to credit the Coast Guard's tactic which impeded and obstructed like the pacifist strategies of protestors. More like chess than open confrontation, later it would be different. The Coast Guard acted as the non-violent wing of the military, but warned that further contact would lead to violent responses.

The submarine in the distance was still not out of reach for blockaders. With binoculars I spotted an aluminum canoe between us and the *Peacemaker*, the two people aboard paddling to the sub with their hands in the water, their sweater sleeves soaking. When we got close, they steered the canoe toward us. I couldn't make out the name they'd carefully painted at the bow in large yellow letters. We handed two paddles over the gray water, their hands pink and freezing white at the knuckles. "God bless you," the man said. We asked where their paddles were. The Coast Guard confiscated them and left the boat to drift. As they waved and began paddling out to the submarine, their yellow name shone on the water: "Lost Children."

Farther out was another small CD boat, a Coast Guard cruiser circling, creating wake powerful enough to put the two demonstrators in the icy water. Here it became clear that while the Coast Guard's intent was to "protect" the submarine by leaving boats stranded and people dunked in Puget Sound, it relinquished its mission to protect citizens and safeguard our waters. The *James Jordan*, a little boat, circled the Trident within twenty feet, chased by Coast Guard boats, and Sunshine Appleby jumped into the water, but the Coast Guard did not arrest her and those aboard. Sunshine, it turns out, had from the beginning been ready to throw herself in the path of the Trident nuclear submarine. She declared she was ready to die to stop it. She came closest to the *Ohio*.

In hindsight I can't remember anyone who seriously believed such a protest could deter the Navy. After a couple of years of protest, letters to the editor, town meetings at which an increased Naval presence in our local waters was decried, many in the communities of Western Washington saw no harmful impact from Trident, while others could enumerate environmental, economic, and safety issues that warranted discussion. At one town meeting a big man took a threatening pose; he mentioned an article in the *Atlantic Monthly* about Vietnam vets living in the wilds of the Olympic Peninsula, vets who might take it into their heads to wage guerrilla war against the Naval bases at Indian Island and Bangor. Harmless Lilliputians, they were not *with* us, as all administrations after 9/11 shall feel entitled to say. When all else failed, heroism was called for, since no one thought the military could be stopped, or changed. The *Peacemaker* evaded until the Coast Guard cutter rammed her. Neither boat was in the restricted zone when *Ohio* crept into the distance beyond feeble protest. The *Point Glass* Coast Guard cutter tied up to the *Peacemaker* and Guardsmen boarded her, civil-disobedience plywood dinghies circling, people screaming at the Coast Guard, calling the names of the captive crew, singing "Happy Birthday." August 2, 1982, was the fifty-second birthday of the mother of the captain of *Point Glass.* Five or six people sat on deck, handcuffed behind their backs, others manacled at their legs. People complained later of a finger clamp which tightened with movement causing their hands to swell and blacken. A Guardsman stood over them with an M16 in his hands. About eighteen, he was nervous and uncomfortable, guarding without conviction. I wonder how he remembers the day he was called upon to act so publicly, though he had not thought through why he was there. He was the age my father was in March, 1945, when he found himself hurling napalm onto the city of Tokyo. Unlike the young man holding the M16 to defend his country from rabid wet protesters, my father prepared for months as a radio operator and gunner for a strike force of three hundred and thirty B-29s under the command of Curtis LeMay. It was his first of thirty missions; between 70,000 and 140, 000 people were incinerated, and he never spoke of it.

Holding the weapon, ready for attack, the young Guardsman was the center of a spectacle of such order and chaos as no one could have anticipated. Boats of all sizes circled the *Peacemaker*, its crew in chains, and the *Point Glass* where more armed young men appeared. In gray fog a woman spoke loudly in slow and pleading tones as her medical boat circled, "They are cold and numb, and need our help," since some of the manacled had been in capsized boats. Overhead three helicopters growled above her voice. News boats circled with cameras and notepads. At the widest circle, Suzuki, a monk from Japan in saffron robe and shaved head, stood high in the bow of a sloop; ghostly and eerily his drum beat accounted for the dead in Hiroshima and Nagasaki, moaning his chant or dirge.

M16 in one hand, in the other a water hose unreeling behind him, another Guardsman yelled for someone to turn on the water. In a tiny civil-disobedience boat at the bow of the *Peacemaker*, one of the protesters was holding in both hands the lines of *Peacemaker* and *Point Glass* while they unleashed the power hose. Those aboard *Peacemaker* bailed furiously, drenched to the skin. On the *Point Glass* the boy with the gun shouted to the protester to let go. From a higher deck, through a megaphone, a Coast Guard officer ordered the line dropped: "This is not a question of peace; this is a question of authority." Authority only, since Trident had passed us by and there was only the crew of this Coast Guard cutter to hold accountable for its collusive abandonment of frightened and determined boaters. He will not let go. Later he told me, David who had grown up on military bases, that over the blast of the power hose he'd heard Coast Guard men calling to the commander like youngsters in a panic, shrill, calling their dad. He seemed prepared to take the dowsing for some time, water blasting down his neck. After about five minutes, he let go, his boat veered away, and the words of the delivery driver come back to me: "They're telling them to get ready for another Chicago."

The Coast Guard cutter began to ease past, the *Peacemaker* tied alongside, taking her to Bangor, her crew on the deck of the *Point Glass* lying on their stomachs, faces calmly peering from behind stanchions, their eyes like those of large captive animals, in shock or pain, having crossed a major river to find there was no return. They were kept on deck nine hours.

We picked up two people in a CD boat, Dot and John from Ashland, Oregon. They called our hot tea a sacrament and spoke of their conviction that everyone was where they were supposed to be, no one a loser: Navy, Coast Guard, or blockaders. They told about John Nelson aboard the *Ploughshares* with Ruth, 1974 Mother of the Year from Edina, Minnesota, seventy-eight years old, with heart problems, nitroglycerine strapped to her wrist. John was an infant when he and his parents survived a German submarine blockade. He had just maneuvered the *Ploughshares* around four Coast guard boats, shutting down his engine when they stopped, gunning it, speeding away until the Coast Guard forced him into illegal waters and arrested him.

On land at Oak Bay everyone told stories and made sure of the safety of others. John Schell had no money and laughed about hitchhiking back to Washington, D.C. He was seventy-four. He came to Oak Bay after five months in jail for pouring blood on the White House. He fasted forty-five days in jail because the name of the Trident sub, *Corpus Christi*, meant the body of Christ. "Justice is eternal, reality is not always truth. The truth is in yourself, but you spend a lot of time searching." I wonder now if we have been on opposite sides of other protests. He had a soft Irish voice, and would have reminded me of my father, whose dream it was to fly to Ireland, except that John was a happy man, and my father, for whom happiness was intermittent, only occasionally escaped the flak coming into his bomb-bay doors, the numbers of those killed, or the memory of camaraderie and respect and duty, and what duty made him believe he had to do. The action delayed the arrival of the submarine, was the way John tallied up the results; there were no losers. His friends were arrested and would be in Superior Court in Seattle, where he would participate in further protests. The location of one man in a rowboat had still to be verified.

For me, the boy with the gun was the big loser. If he is alive today, he is not talking about these events. He is not telling his children or his grandchildren. My speculation is he did not last much longer in the Coast Guard, nor join another branch of the military. He had strong feelings about the WTO protesters in Seattle, much more bizarre and belligerent than those suburban families on the water around him. He's annoyed and bothered by the millions of marchers all over the planet condemning America in Iraq and Afghanistan, though he may no longer support the war. He stays home and raises a family or lives alone, bitter. He will not speak of it.

My father also never spoke about war, never gave details. Never mentioned he had the Distinguished Flying Cross, The Air Medal, and an Airman of the Year award. Once he did say war was a horrible thing. When he worked sixty hours a week at two different jobs, my mother found in his dresser drawer a stash of Benzedrine, Kerouac's drug, upper of choice for long-haul road trips, and used by radio operators in the Pacific Theatre of World War II, but not to be used by the gunners. Radio operators like him needed to stay awake flying reconnaissance missions or reporting weather. No drug helped him undo the effect of flying low-elevation bombing missions like the fire-bombing of Tokyo.

When I found his medals in the dresser drawer, two folded-up newspaper articles had been pressed inside the case. One was "On This Day," from the November 24, 1991, edition of the *Boston Globe*. William F. Buckley was 67, Marlin Fitzwater was 50; Charles Darwin had published *Origin of Species* on that day; the battle of Lookout Mountain began in Tennessee, and Jack Ruby shot Lee Harvey Oswald some 28 years earlier. Those events had lines drawn through them, but the date itself was circled, a signal to me; the boy who held that rifle will leave a torn bit of newsprint for his firstborn. Down the page, 1944 was circled and the words: "U.S. bombers based on Saipan attacked Tokyo in what was the first raid against the Japanese capital by land-based planes." In the margin was his own firm and distinctive printing: "Mission #1—29 to go." Not much to pick up on there, except that he left no written or verbal judgment of this or any of his missions. The other clipping is more revealing. "March 9-10" is circled as well as "70,000 lives —possibly as many as 140,000." As well as the paragraph: "They would countenance the obliteration of every Japanese city if it could prevent a slaughter of US troops on foreign beaches. And that is what Gen. Curtis Lemay*, B-29 commander in the Pacific, proceeded to do. His planes struck Nagoya two days later, then Osaka, Kobe, and back to Tokyo twice more. By the end of the war, the B-29s would level 178 square miles of urban areas and kill 330,000 people. Hiroshima and Nagasaki were spared fire-bombing only to await the atomic bomb that would at last shock the Japanese into surrender." From these words he circled are arrows pointing to his writing: "I was there."

---

*When reflecting on the campaign after the war, some expressed doubts about the morality of the firebombing. Curtis LeMay later said: "I suppose if I had lost the war, I would have been tried as a war criminal."

SILVER SEA

Passing through Ballard Locks, I don't know how to describe the craving I feel at the bow of the *Silver Sea,* as we slide down walls of intensely green algae, gulls haunting the air. To them we become small as the water leaves the locks, lowers us to sea level—thalassa, green algae, muck on the surface, pleasure boats at moorage in the harbor, on our way to the sea lands, ship wake, ferry traffic, gull road, salmon-leaping paths.

After a while, in my bunk reading, I hear a squeak like music. I'm proud I could recognize the sound. We have tied up to a purse seiner, fenders sing on gunwales. Donovan and Sherman will hoist salmon into our boat while I keep records and watch so I can spell one of them when the next boat comes. They put on slickers resolutely in the middle of the night. Sardonically grim, they strap on valor, chastened by what is to be done. As they work, even as they joke with the captain of the seiner, they pass precious cargo, yet brusquely slap fish on deck leaving a shine there. There are blood drops everywhere, even on my sweater though I sit in the cabin recording in pencil the number and weights they call out of Brights and Darks, Chum and King. Once, on deck for a breather, I saw a fish fall alive overboard and escape.

In the industrial and romantic glare of seiner light, some of the crew fillet fish, some pass them, huge ten- or twenty-pound salmon, eyes wide and elegant. It's a factory at sea. The Greek word, *thalassa,* reminds me of an old poem, not Homer's but William Cullen Bryant's "Thanatopsis," death, and earth its containment.

On the *Paragon,* the seiner, fish are alive in the ship's hold. Turning them over to us, the buyer's boat, they drain the hold and hundreds, hundreds, of fish thrash, writhe, splash, and bang against one another racing to follow the water out. Then men go down and put them on deck, lifting gently, not to bruise, each sacramental fish into our arms. In the box, weighed and counted for market, they still thrash, until, dumped on ice, the spirit finally leaves. Having been kept alive so long, they make the freshest servings. Fish blood turns the surface of Shilshole Bay scarlet. A skiff slides across blackened foam and scales; someone going to the bar for last call. I watch the white wake of *Alaska Blues,* another seiner, stripe the black water. November will be the month for chum, its skipper told me. He's been fishing Alaska, where they have had a good season: we're not. I close the door to the hold where they flap to death, eyes red open.

Under the sign of "Cash Buyer," our competitor, skipper of *Myrna Rose,* has painted a shamrock on his wheelhouse. He comes over the VHF. His name is Bud Royal. "This is the *Myrna Rose.*" He says what he'll pay for bright, not dark, red chum, or dogs, up to five thousand pounds. Then says he'll only buy from gill netters, who won't be in until early in the morning. He will fillet what he buys and send the fish by air to San Francisco, that's what Donovan guesses. But when I ask Bud where he does send them, he says, "Texas!" Working for himself and not a company the way Donovan does, he can pay any price he wants, but now that he has announced well in advance, he has raised the stakes for all buy-boats. Donovan doesn't want to get on the VHF to confer with his boss because he'd be announcing to everyone in the fleet that he has this problem. So we must row in to a pay phone. This might be an elaborate excuse to head for the bar. He says most gill netters won't come in before dawn, and anyone who shows up before midnight doesn't have shit.

We get into the dinghy like a pair of smugglers. I row of course, and try to keep the oars quiet as possible, which seems stupid since Donovan's laughing at his own jokes makes us as conspicuous as an outboard motor. Sherman is content to stay on board with his dog Higgins, whom I am just as glad to be getting away from.

I don't remember how we got back on board. I must have rowed again, and I'm sure we were pretty noisy. We didn't leave the bar until closing, and Donovan got word from his boss to price just below Bud. At dawn I don't feel well, and the first gill netters tie up to us, thick as flies: The *Ballerina, Twin Sisters*, and *Astro*. On deck, a cup of Sherman's gritty coffee in hand, I'm swimming in fish. They sail into the weight bucket. Even dizzy, I feel the romance of the salmon, but different from last night under the lights of purse seiners. As I unload, I remember my dream of seeing a big submarine go past us starboard, too small to have been a Trident. A bigger one did go by, and we all saw, in the gray pre-dawn.

After the wave of gill netters subsides, the Washington State Fisheries biologist comes on board. He decides how many fish go to Indians, how many to whites, how long it should take for Indians to get their allotted percentage of the catch, and for whites to catch up, and vice-versa. Each boat has to sell all its fish, can't keep any, but the buyer can sell fish back to the fisher. Because some fishermen keep their own fish to take home, although it is illegal, the biologist can't estimate the total catch and can't decide allotments of fishing days. Sports fishermen take the biggest percentage of unrecorded fish, and sell to restaurants, also illegal. Little private buyers like Bud Royal represent another big percentage because by the time the biologist comes along and tries to record, Bud's gone.

Two men stand on deck and discuss the deaths of friends. They are unsentimental and laugh sadly. Donovan tells me the story of the *Alki*, his own boat which he sold to two "children" helped in the purchase by an elderly man in Anacortes. The man gave them whatever thousands of dollars and took an I.O.U. He wanted to go to Alaska one last time. When he fell overboard, they got the boat and who the hell knows where they are now.

Somewhere in Alaska with or without the *Alki*, they got right with the Lord and who knows maybe they don't even owe the estate anything anymore. "Full fathom five thy father lies; . . . Those are pearls that were his eyes."

I sit on deck most of the time in transit. A group of orcas raced the *Silver Sea* yesterday. Black and white flashes cut across the bow. On the stern now while Donovan, Sherman, and Higgins are in the wheelhouse, I imagine myself afloat on the wake. I can't grab anything; they can't hear me. I wave; they move away faster and I can't swim. My boots drag me down, my clothes heavy, arms cold; the wake bubbles into my mouth and tastes bad. I choke for twenty minutes before they are a speck.

The fishermen's faces are haggard and hard, heroic like Odysseus. *Hercules*, the tug, pulls a barge big as a floating skyscraper. The captain of the *Brenda Rose*, a young man with a face that's lived a century, heads down the Duwamish. I wave to him as his boat passes us. Donovan tells me get back to cleaning the deck. I say I did already. No, he says, there's a lot of minor blood-scrubbing left. Luckily Higgins, who hasn't left the boat, hasn't pissed or shit in three days. I stay on deck because the wheelhouse smells of cigarettes, exhaust gasoline, and fish blood.

By the time we're ready to walk on pavement, or, as we've been saying for days, to "get the fuck off the boat," the boss calls; there's another opening on Hood Canal, another day or two for white commercial fishermen to haul in everything they find. It means another ten thousand pounds of fish and maybe a hundred dollars for me. "Maybe five hundred, maybe a thousand," Donovan says. So far I've made eighty-eight dollars. Greed competes with exhaustion; I tell myself I don't want the money that much but it's no use.

The competition is incredible, the opening a secret. We arrive too late, the catch already sold. We beat them last week, Donovan says, and they beat us this week. After we sit for hours waiting for gill netters to sell us some fish, we take what we have back to the fish buyer's pier. From Hood Canal off Whiskey

Spit, we head for the Duwamish River, cluttered with shipbuilders. In among moorages is Booth Fisheries, which buys not only salmon, but apples, wheat, anything they're brought. I'm told they own the Northwest. A guy at a bar one night told me, "Hang around Donovan Dundin long enough and you'll see everything there is to see about how the Northwest works."

This is how it works: I shovel a ton and a half of ice and unload eight thousand pounds of salmon. Saturated by the bodies of swimmers, I remember how they pass without dignity into the huge bucket the buyer lowers into our hold and hoists up to fillet, ice, and sell. Thousands of iced open eyes look at me in the hold; I grow panicky in the small tight place. I think about the totem of good harvest, and sit down on the remaining ton of slippery fish.

As soon as we unload, we head for the Wharf Tavern and I begin spending the few dollars I draw against wages which will not amount to much. We drink to somebody's birthday; everyone lifts a drink bought with a hundred dollar bill. A man from Las Vegas is up on stage; he's never gone out on the water, but his entire audience has. He croons late Fifties tunes, wearing a sequined shirt, fish scales open to the chest. It's one of the saddest stage routines I ever saw.

THE LAND, THE BOYCOTT &THE UNARMED MUSE

Land is our economy turned inward. We like to bring everything out. Stone turns to statue, we flatten metal into coin. A very small person with a fine hammer chips away at old veins in the dark, building where only the earth builds, where magma glow is the only light, chipping uninterested in the coming and going of anyone else, heedless of the worm, keeper of the last word.

Darkness is the house soil built. Nothing but the spoiled wealth of an earlier inhabitant is there, and the strata of our needs built on the forgotten, the fine secret so grainy and moist the hand won't touch. Yet the mining continues: bits of rock, soft immaculate desires, dust from the dry door of the soul.

I came digging with a stick in a hole to find precious metals. At some point I climbed out and looked around. I would have had to die to enter the ground. Even Orpheus the living could not pull his treasure out. It's sad because I want to enter the ground. I am stranded on the surface of a planet and unable to root, and very far, very far.

Metals lie hereabouts taken from the ground, the halo of purpose about them. I imagine hands worked them and time to time touch steel, run a finger over chrome. Fine soil sifts to the bottom of a hole. What was hollow gets filled. Whatever is needed can't be far. What was taken reasserts itself.

Economics is a sacred science: *oikos*, house; *nemein*, to manage. The house is not for sale because the inhabitants have nowhere else. No one is ashamed of the dirt, built effortlessly by birth, rot, renewal . Mostly dream, womb, cozy lap of soil, breast of bedrock. One takes, one gives. Enough. Inside is the perfection of the State.

118

At first soil didn't appeal to men. Grass and weeds were nothing. The pull of the ground made us afraid, our houses got bigger. "I own this land from the corner marker in a line to that one there, to that one north of us, and west to the one just above, and back here again. My land forms a square. It's all I need."

Today the real-estate agent came to see the house. He's heard it's for sale and showed it to a nice couple from the city. He didn't knock, never stopped asking the price of furniture and figuring the value per board foot of the stand of cedar. I said the wind was nice. The couple wiped their feet; they liked the northwest exposure. It was raining. The agent didn't remove his sunglasses.

Easter we planted trees close to Forks. I stopped to look at the line of fir seedlings, and thought they spelled in code something for hawks cruising the clear-cut. I lay on the slope to have lunch, a wren squeaking out a song from the burn piles. The planting was unsatisfying. How did the slope plant? How could I plant like the slope? How could I become the slope? What doctor takes these seeds to their brothers and sisters? The wind? What is straight? What is pattern?

The entire sky moved over me. Even the hawks were still. In heaven an old woman stepped from her house to gather sticks from the floor of a cloud. She looks so cool up there, small as a feather. And we—we are in the field. We shade our eyes. We wave.

THE DUCKABUSH, THE DOSEY, AND THE HAMMA HAMMA

When we arrived in late afternoon, Steve went swimming where the river pooled, low for June. "Come on in." It was too cold for me. An ouzel dipped in and out the rocks downstream. Now I was up to my knees fording the river, leaning on a stick, prodding a bottom rock, then another, dragging my feet through the current. Steve sat under an alder, smiling, camera in his lap. Eddies circled my thighs and moved reluctantly on. I thought I'd be knocked down, the way the current shot. I picked my way doggedly, tennis shoes dangling from a belt loop, shirt like a bandanna around my head, when Steve took the first picture.

Across the river the floor of the woods was nothing but green. We were in elk feeding grounds. No one crossed over, not hikers who stayed on the trails, or fishermen who worked the bank. Maybe the elk already had our scent; Steve said if we covered ourselves with a harmless scent, we could walk among them. We were staring into the river, Steve squatting, camera in one hand. Neither of us knew little songs to attract the animal. Still, there had to be a way to find elk. We knew our presence was a trespass which a good photo of elk could justify. Once I saw a herd switch-back a clear-cut hill. I could at first see only white tails, flanks the same as burnt ground, until one moved. Another time I came upon a small herd in the middle of a trail not ten feet in front of me. After a few minutes, Steve went up the elk trail toward the old-growth cedar.

In a meadow near twinflower and starflowers, I looked around for a place to sit, stepping gingerly in bare feet among red dots in moss and mushroom sprouts, wet beds where the sun hit. Small twinflower bells hung in delicate bunches over

120

the ground and it was hard to sit without trampling. I found a flat rock and immediately began identifying. I had learned names of certain flowers and insects, which were difficult to develop an interest in, and the nomenclature was strange. Earlier that day, I disturbed a fat bee inside a white foxglove; it flew the zebra pattern up the petal.

The purpose of our group was to seek protection for part of the Duckabush River, under the aegis of National Park System, which itself arose through the efforts of visionaries who underestimated the greed of American industry. In 1832, when Congress received its first request for a national park, George Caitlin told the American people that setting aside portions of wilderness would create a kind of museum in which "the world could see for ages to come, the native Indian in his classic attire, galloping his wild horse, with sinewy bow, and shield and lance, amid the fleeting herds of elk and buffaloes." A romance certainly, given the history of white-versus-native relations, but the great Western artist was sincere in his desire to preserve a way of life evaporating as the western push steadily depleted herds. It wasn't until 1872 that the world's first national park was established, at Yellowstone. It's difficult to understand the purpose of setting aside portions rather than demanding limits on progress. Only eighteen years later, after failing to see the world as George Caitlin had, the government sent troops to South Dakota against the Sioux at Wounded Knee. Black Elk's words about that disaster echo the horror of William Butler Yeats in Ireland and Chinua Achebe in Africa: "There is no center any longer." In 1973 the Oglala Sioux seized Wounded Knee to protest treaty violations and demand the United States give back the land called "Pahasapa," the Black Hills.

Raymond Dasmann was the first to use the term "bioregions" to reconsider placing arbitrary boundaries around wilderness. Boundaries are changes found in habitat. In the 1850s G.P. Marsh spoke against deforestation and the misuse of lands, citing disappeared native grasses in California, hardwoods in the

East, Southern farmlands abandoned, eroded and infertile, wildlife slaughtered in vast numbers everywhere. In the 1890s the first national forests were established and forestry management concepts were applied to cutting and replanting trees.

The last time I was in Yellowstone National Park, I saw a buffalo and a herd of small elk come to be photographed at the side of the road. At least it looked to me and the other tourists as if they came to be photographed, a classic American assumption. I had been through the Black Hills and the buffalo were thin and small, still mythic but domestic and ignoble. I sat on the breezy veranda of some resort overlooking the very hill where Black Elk had visions, and I ate a buffalo burger while on the television at the bar inside Ronald Reagan became the Republican Party's nominee for the first time.

Making notes so as to understand the fragility of the meadow, I was reduced to terminology: bunchberry, flowering dogwood, Indian pipe, salal, columbine, buttercup, sword fern, lady fern, bracken, maidenhair, lichens and Oregon grape, thimbleberry, veronica, foam flower, bunchberry again, queen's cup, wild ginger, bedstraw, monkey flower, goat's beard, saxifrage. I walked back to the edge of the river, notes in a pack. One of our group had gone down this river in a wetsuit through icy rapids. He told me about swimming beside salmon, and holding one. I wondered if the natives of this area swam here. The reason parks have so much difficulty surviving, if they survive intact at all, is that surrounding devastation gets inside in the process of deculturation; a people assimilate the natives of a place they wish to inhabit. Raymond Dassman says: "Biosphere people created national parks. Ecosystem people have always lived in the equivalent of a national park. It is the kind of country that ecosystem people have always protected, that biosphere people want to have formally reserved and safeguarded. But, of course, first the ecosystem people must be removed."

In the Black Hills, I stopped at Mount Rushmore. In sunglasses, camera around my neck, hundreds of Bermuda shorts going by beneath rows of state flags, I noticed the bumper sticker on an old pickup leaving the parking lot: "The Black Hills Are Not for Sale." The Sioux claimed they still owned the Black Hills, even that mountain, all that blind stone, where both Bush administrations have actually threatened to add the inane smile of Ronald Reagan.

On the path the winds were rushing in the salal and young fir. My ear had grown used to the deafening river. The path was small and the very large tracks of elk were perfect as sculpture. Still barefoot, I walked above the trail to avoid leaving tracks where elk walked. Although our tracks couldn't mean anything to them—they had our scent already—we had decided to attempt to leave this side of the river as unchanged as possible. Soon the path turned all rock and climbed to a clearing full of white phlox and strawberry and small Indian paintbrush.

Steve was on a large boulder, his camera held toward basalt cliffs and a ridge which twisted about this bowl, Jupiter Ridge, five or six thousand feet. He pointed out Saint Peter's Dome behind us; beyond one ridge was the Dosewallips, or Dosey watershed, and beyond the other the Hamma Hamma. The prospect of a dam on this river made people afraid of the government. The price of real estate was expected to go down, and many thought they would have to move off land that had been in their families for generations. The alternative to moving was to have the business of the dam as your neighbor. Fortunately, the dam project did not proceed. The failure of a park is that some of a river can be protected if it falls within the arbitrary boundary, the headwaters of the Duckabush River for instance, but not the estuary where that river enters Hood Canal. There is a line between the National Forest and the National Park. The former may be logged, dammed, or mined; the latter may not.

It's possible to kill a river from the neck down by cutting off its rights to protection with a simple bill. Yet we were standing in the watershed—the entire river, including St. Peter's Dome and Jupiter Ridge, whatever was moving and falling. All of this could be reduced to a trickle in a sink, or the assurance of a stream into dishwashers. Standing in an unprotected yet intact watershed, an entirely unique place, we could recognize that what was pitiless and prehistoric formed elk, peregrine falcon, salmon, and dipper. In such a place even those who are not extremists can see why people might chain themselves to a tree or a rock in futile protest of flooding or logging. Most of us don't think it normal to live high up a redwood to protect it. Though we want the world the way it is, we don't see the resemblance to the Sioux at Wounded Knee or the Black Hills.

When we walked out to the river through old growth we saw bear tracks, so Steve talked loud. Elk tracks beside the river in the sand, frogs in small pools. We heard owls and grouse. We were about to recross the river at a shallow place. I was standing on a boulder looking into the quick small currents. Steve was in a pool near shore, sun ricocheting off blurred arrow-headed waves. He whispered, pointing upstream into the sunlight. In the glare, only the pale column of its neck. Lifting his camera, he raised one foot onto a slippery ledge. No good. Got higher on the rock, the view better. The animal lifted its head from drinking. Certainly this was rare. A small plane ground above us, its shadow swept the river. The elk turned and drew into the dark and the trees.

CLIMATE & CURRENCY

I was working in Boston as a laborer most of the summer, but I lost that job by admitting my lifelong fear of heights while atop a four-story ladder unable to let go long enough to move a paint brush over brownstone window trim. I got another job soon, working in the hottest days for a young contractor overburdened with clients. When I arrived Friday of the third week, no one was there. All week the crew had bet against Karl making payroll. On Tuesday they told me to look out the window onto the docks of Boston Harbor: a big guy with long hair was hooking my precious little Saab beater to his tow truck. By the time he climbed into his cab, I had the chain off my front bumper and shot away. That was the car I'd rebuilt from tattered Xeroxed manuals, and intended to drive back to Washington. So that was a bad day; I should have recognized the signs. On Wednesday, he laid off the secretary; by Thursday the crew was tense.

But on Friday, faithful as ever, I was mixing paint, cleaning rollers, putting on overalls. By noon still alone, I sat eating lunch as a man in a black business suit entered the room. "Wet Paint," I said through a mouthful of peanut butter. He set his sparkling leather briefcase on the plastic tarp over the kitchen counter, and asked for Karl. His Boston accent, the rich and flagrant "a" of "Kahl," of all my youthful vowels the most sincere, reminded me how I'd replaced it with that harsh Western "ar," our ubiquitous standard. He began telling me, and I couldn't gather why, that Karl was deeply in debt, had backed out of contracts, was being sued for everything he and his family owned. I continued eating till the man left, closed the paint cans tightly, and went home.

When I arrived at Karl's house that night, the neighbor across the street stepped onto his porch, holding paycheck envelopes Karl, who'd gone into hiding, paid him to distribute. Mine was attached to a note, "Mike, this is all I have now, the rest next week. I sorry." I sorry? Fifty dollars, and he owed me three hundred. I staked out his house for a week, leaving conciliatory notes and my mother's phone number. One night, voice muffled like a man in a dark closet, he said he'd hire me for this really big job.

I worked for Karl that winter and spring remodeling an old brick building in downtown Boston. He hired one or two friends he hadn't screwed yet, from the old neighborhood. He paid what he owed me in installments as we gutted and framed; at lunch we watched dust float out the door and onto the shoulders of accountants and secretaries. He said he called me, not the rest of the crew, because I left the note. A note would have never occurred to those boys who hadn't shown up Friday. I thought I knew them. Their accents and Karl's were from my own neighborhood, but I had moved away long ago, and self-conscious of being tagged by my voice, I emulated sharper, more unassuming enunciations. I knew too that because I was a stranger, and no longer native, I could suggest there was a right thing to do without making a threat. Natives of a place may expect more, or give in to outrage when politicians or fellow citizens commit wrong. The outsider assumes through a universal principle that change should occur, but the native, affronted by negative behavior, accepts his losses, vows revenge, or throws up his hands and looks for work elsewhere.

The root of "native," and "nature," *natura* in Latin, comes up from the ground. Like native products we nailed together from Maine, Vermont, and Quebec forests, these boys came from a climate either the cause or the effect of granite hills, brittle sun, deciduously quilted sidewalks, clipped verbs, and blunt manners. They knew the language of payback. I never found out how they approached him, or how Karl paid them off, but some currency must have changed hands. They knew his parents after all; they'd recognize his car. One phone call and they'd have shown up on our downtown site to haul away tools or break windows. Come to think of it, he might have given them his car. Why else was I called into service as driver every morning? Sometimes his girlfriend squeezed in, the recently laid-off secretary spilling coffee and smoking through the crawl of traffic to an office near a tunnel. Once, when the Saab broke down on the Southeast Expressway, we were pulled over, the hood up, when a steaming old Chrysler rattled in behind us. The driver and passenger, burly guys in shabby parkas, stood over the engine a minute, more to commiserate than offer a lift. Then, after they'd already said goodbye and good luck, they were sorry but they were almost out of gas and could they hit us up for a couple bucks?

Currency is why we have jobs. Yet so much goes to getting there, not to mention investments in consumables to contain the restless spirit. Currency is the roll we pull out, the rock that translates weather rendered as milled planks and labored into local prizes. In an interdependent world the fair exchange is an offline elite of supply, demand, and trust. When Europeans discovered interdependent native communities among inhabitants of the New World, they created dentalia factories to subvert the economy. Dentalia shells, already in use in trade between tribes, became inflated and were superseded by the coin of the realm.

Some transactions require the buyer to decide a thing's worth, a gamble if he was outside of the "current," so to speak; the seller must choose among strangers' offerings—which stone, or tree bark, pelt, shell, fish is worth which commodity. Europeans witnessed this. The white trader who dealt in blankets and alcohol, guns and gingham, even the humiliation of hats and uniforms after the buffalo was removed, had to value and determine barter, and had to know his customer. He had to know he supplied only what natives needed to live with whites who wanted them gone, to supply commodities and teach consumerism; supply and demand led to replacement currencies in the pacification of the West.

When Karl found out I wrote poetry, he mocked me for the low-paying art form, as I waited for him to buy *Lotto* tickets. He forgot the remark, avidly scraping metallic dust with a dirty fingernail to reveal a three-dollar winning number. I watched him slip the card into his wallet and smile about his lucky streak. "I won ten dollars yesterday." He didn't redeem *Lotto* winnings, and had a stash of silver cards. Maybe little cards saved in wallets, or glove compartments, cupboards or libraries as tacky bookmarks, will be valuable not for their redemptive qualities, but for their colors, or numbers, or as symbols of exchange in some *Mad Max* post-apocalypse or *Lord of the Flies* island.

Karl was too cagey to have gone to war. Had the draft been instituted when he turned eighteen, he'd have managed to keep from seeing service. He was a young man who wanted to make money, and war would have been too distracting. Those young men of his first crew, though, would have been cannon fodder. Too young for Vietnam and too old when the Gulf War came along, what they did when not in Karl's fruitless employ involved petty theft and brawling. They would have lived their entire lives outside Boston in Dorchester or Southie. Through family pressures and lack of foresight, they would breed. There would be one currency, and they would slave to amass as much as their wives or the courts demanded.

When Karl mocked notoriously ill-paid poets, he spoke for them too. He spoke from his neighborhood, two little antagonistic communities, Dorchester and Southie, where my parents were born, where I was native, where I learned what they had learned: poetry is not for men. Having left their birthplaces, to the extent anyone is capable, some poets find in striving to perfect their native dialects a currency to spend perhaps in bars and on certain streets in rain and wind where those who pass would themselves give up all their wealth for a chance to declaim. Maybe it was the same with migrating people who performed stories and songs to keep alive what they were leaving. But Karl's crew, no. Whatever they were leaving was the same as where they were going. Currency didn't change because risk didn't. What makes poetry and language akin to currency is that someone risks offering it, risks rejection. What we bring from our native places may be valued, not for how like it is to the familiar poetics and the local ear, but how new, and with what courage it must be brought forth. It is a kind of war, this contest in the arena of public art. We become self-conscious, but we affirm that consciousness is not delusion and we are not mad. We compete with ourselves and others to be different or alike. Currency as language gives away our influences, origins, and predecessors. For stamps of approval from peers and strangers, we knock off formal poems keeping in notes our more dangerous opinions of the world.

When North American tribes interacted, they created currency. When they left native soil, following a herd, crop depletion, or a change of weather, the means of exchange may have been gifts. Yet the Northwest potlatch, for instance, wasn't always enjoyable gift-giving. The competition at potlatches defined the greatest personal and tribal wealth by the most abundant giving. The belief that one could gather more from the surroundings than anyone else led to sometimes deadly contests. Native peoples, after the creation of the New World, failed initially as economic entities because they did not anticipate how through cupidity, one could take what was already free by calling it property. The potlatch exemplified wealth consciousness before wealth eroded. The replacement value of goods offered by white societies created an untenable materialism when a resource like buffalo still flourished and the hunt gave communities strength. Other currencies arose as Indians were pushed farther away from lands they were used to. Just as Europeans brought more than they needed to survive, and could bestow what they considered trinkets, so tribes pushing into new territories brought products of their native climates, prized far away because they fit in the palm of a hand and enlarged the world. Much as Odysseus, bearing an object on his shoulder, walked inland till someone asked, "Is that a tool for winnowing?" "An oar," he said and began work on the altar and the slaughter of bulls far from an ocean that had until then been unimagined.

Born of plenty, currency represents precious, rare, and distant climates. Yet Incas valued gold for aesthetic reasons and abundance, and had no need to trade until Hernan Cortez recognized it as the foundation of wealth and established the currency of New Spain. Gold from Incan gift exchange and ornaments in blood sacrifice enabled the establishment of a European division of wealth and labor, and was worth the destruction of a race. The entire history of the subversion of native economies in the New World took place before what Albert Camus calls the advent of modern times, 1789. The French Revolution began the "history of nations," and ended the history of Divine Right. The will of God, through the infallible conduits of the rulers of Europe, commanded that native races on this continent be subjugated or eliminated, and the societal structure of Europe emulated. The plan to subvert native economies wasn't difficult to implement; Cortez could have used it had bloodshed not been his mission. Prior to his arrival, the Incas may have traveled and used gold as currency, but such occasions would have been rare.

Crossing the Sea of Cortes

The Sea of lifts and rolls,
the body of a whale rides thousands
of swells. Moon touches the horizon,
and we, on the M. M. Puerto V.,
we ride these wastes.

Lovers on deck walk like us.
They steal into shadow.
We stand at the rail.

A star is on the Sea of Cortes.

We watch it race, the sudden prey of sharks
upon the waves, until we see it is a hand,
palm up, lying on a swell. It drifts
into the foam, until we see it is a face.

We turn so quickly from the rail
the lovers lift their eyes.

We turn back, and watch it float,
eyes shut, folded in moon.

We make ourselves leave the rail.
The lovers walk before us
to find a place to lie.

Cortes, long ago, was a god returning,
his hair prophecy's last detail.

Moctezuma sent a legion of his best.

Hernan returned each man's right hand.

Now only moon shatters the swells.

The heart of a young man is a thin reed pipe.

In two years he destroyed the Aztecs.

Tonight families lie on blankets

131

on the floor of the salon.
Why have I come here?

To see a man and woman
roll and fall into one another,
his hand on her hip?

The morning sun
counts dimes
on their spines.
In waves the light
is a bird, great Condor,
splashing where the lost
map floats.

*

I quit working for Karl in the spring of 1980, and left Boston in my rusted Saab, forest green, crammed with books and tools. In San Francisco, I haunted City Lights Bookstore for a while to read yet another biography or lost manuscript by my fellow Massachusetts native, Jack Kerouac. Yet his search for humanity became finally too depressing, and the writings of Beats and the Beat-driven so chaotic I sought a language less obsessed with frailty, less on the edge of collapse from anxiety. One summer afternoon at Vesuvio's, I was reading poets who responded to the horror of a constellation of tyrannies our government supported. Men in naval uniforms were down the bar. At corner tables sat artists and poets, their clothing a giveaway, down to the spray of magenta in a woman's hair, turquoise dripped across black shoes. It was noisy, traffic out the door honking. People seemed excited, as if they might flood the street or take over the government. There was nearly a fight between some guys at the end of the bar, growling like dogs when a hooker bought a pack of cigarettes. From the other side of the room a man stood at his table, shouting loud enough to have silenced the rest of the room, "Coin of the realm? This is what I want for coin of the realm!" A knife out very quickly, he sliced along his slim forearm to his elbow where blood sprinkled his white shirt.

Concerns about peace then were widespread, everybody's business, but now, when retirement waves its dreamy handkerchief across tall grass, peace is the burden only of secretaries of state, men and women who justify their presence on earth by shuttling among warmongers. There have been Secretaries of War, Secretaries of Defense, but so far no Secretaries of Peace, Dennis Kucinich notwithstanding. His proposal of such a position struck voters as a charming, even a novel idea, but not feasible given the state of the world. Though we have Peacekeepers and Officers of the Peace, the politics of interdependent contradictions relies on intimidation as well as the degradation of indigenous currencies. We enforce the peace of the good life, affordable to the qualified; one qualification is flawless defense, a technology sweeping each life on the planet. The Secretaries meet on behalf of peace, and shape language like swords into ploughshares and back into missiles. The communiqués of ambassadors and terrorists are framed as media of exchange, microchips storing till time ends the dialectics of international gift-giving, the back and forth of peacekeeping's labor, the currency of history.

Yet when communities were self-sufficient, the practical means of exchange could have been worked out within the local framework; a regional currency could have been used if suppliers and consumers were mutually dependent. When people left their community, they developed other needs, or discovered suppliers elsewhere whose bias toward the individual created imbalances. "The horn of the rhinoceros," says Gary Snyder, "was prized as material for a beautiful wine cup, the powdered horn greatly valued as an antidote to poison. So the rhinoceros is no longer found in China and illegal poaching today on rhinoceros preserves in India is for the Chinese market. . .Sitka deer were exterminated for antlers-in-velvet for medicine . . . alligators for drum skins."

Its roar gave value to the shell. Currency in Paleolithic Europe and on the steppes of Russia signified rarity; magical uses of the conch were of value, and red ochre for its magic among the Mojave, the Apache, and Australian aborigines. Traded, but not used as common currency, it was a symbol of blood. Pearls had store value; jade, a water symbol, was currency where abundant as in Mexico. Teeth were currency in the Americas and Oceania, where hunting remnants survive as magic. Crystal, the shaman's tool, was somehow not of this world, for all its allure. It resists the ground of our planet, resists shattering in the manner we would have it shatter. Common stones were valuable for their resemblances to animal or human shapes, a fetishistic currency, "Amazon fetishes" used for magic and medicinal power, personal power; feathers for headdresses, seen in rock paintings from ten thousand years ago in Europe and New England, as magic-religious ritual. By the Bronze Age, man the metal-worker began to lose interest in the functions of currency that prevailed in the Paleolithic. As cloth, tools, and weapons advanced, the exchange became more secular.

I left California and came back to the Pacific Northwest, thinking I would peddle what skills I'd picked up on construction sites in downtown Boston. I wanted to hang sheetrock and tape walls, finding sites in various states of remodel. With smooth coats of "mud" I could spread more or less evenly, and days sanding bumps and ridges, which became endless shadows on well-lit surfaces, I figured I could support myself. But I lost money every time out. My meditations on the nature of rock and mud made them glamorous, the primitive evolving under my hand. Words like "dust," or "smooth," or "feather coat," "dimple a screw," "sister a stud," helped me escape the obvious: we earn a living apart from metaphor. Language lulled me to imagine man finds from rock and dirt the wherewithal to build a home, or base an exchange. Currency arises from the principles of production and distribution, opposing forces enabling my servitude and membership in the chain of slaves, which include those geniuses who built the pyramids but could not organize.

I gave up my attempt at independent contractorship to rejoin old friends in our local tree planters' collective, a job I'd once found so grueling I swore I'd never do it again. With my own tools, trained as a carpenter and a specialist in walls, I had been sure I was off and running in the marketplace of competitive skilled labor. Disillusionment was not the recognition that enslavement permeated momentary stays against oppressive self-employment, but the knowledge that we are never independent.

Our little collective contracted to plant trees for the U.S. Forest Service, Weyerhaeuser, and other timber conglomerates. We were part of the long line of producers who put houses where once were woodlands in towns anxiously stumbling behind their growth rates. And the distributors, a smaller and smaller elite, became millionaires because they owned what they would never make. We would go into slash piles and dig eight-inch deep holes, plant a tree perfectly, its roots all hanging down not up, or "j," under dirt we tamped in ten seconds, and jumped out of fallen alder—industrial waste of clear-cutting, often consumed by napalm—to perform the same operation ten feet away, and again, and again. Good planters averaged a thousand trees a day. I did that one day, which may have been part of my reluctance to return; usually paid per tree, my more often six hundred trees a day weren't paying as well as my friends in better shape and inured to endless rain in comfortable campers and portable shacks.

Once I stumbled through slash in cork boots and planted one more tree. I was almost at the road and ready for lunch— peanut butter sandwiches and an orange. A beautiful green stone, almost jade, caught my attention. Currency came to mind. One might have offered this, or a string of these for a night's lodging, for salmon, a bar of soap. Yet, even as I held it in my muddy glove, it turned gray and dirty, ugly and common. So ugly I threw it away and trudged off to eat lunch. On another day I walked in the road full of common rocks, strange shapes of wood, burnt black or gray and dry with the weather of upper elevations where everything is currency—in and of Heraclites's current. Change the only constant, these stones or pieces of petrified wood fluctuate in value, as could the funny rubber industrial artifacts loggers drop and unintentionally frame within the shattered sacred grove—a yellow glove ripped at the thumb beside a newly opened trillium. They are absolutely worthless, but the photographer, the painter who notices them, or the collagist gathering images, defines "primitive" as us. Currency is what turns to significance by resemblance, as stones shaped like pigs or hunters, gold the sweat of the sun, and silver, Incan tears of the moon.

When we came down from the timber industry's high-elevation clear-cuts and looked for ways to spend money, many of us went to artists who crafted with precious stones, feathers, and junk. I have a peregrine falcon in silver with a garnet for an eye. Once I had a money clip made of Mexican silver the shape of a quetzal bird and snake; such magic shapes required self-regulation. Recognizing a vision of the world, the artist captures those who hear without effort, who excuse no imperfection, who act without self-interest or false humility. Blindness and self-importance trap the fruits of a climate within the lines of real estate. If everything could be seen to be alive, or have a spirit, as James Hillman says, we would live within abundance; everything we exchange, the price we shell out for solitude within sheet rock walls, a vital currency. Land and climate create wealth and nothing else. The very notion of a deed which allows us to do anything we want to our property impoverishes the entitled. Yet ownership is temporal, and mortgages, investments, the credit system itself, the last potlatch. We outdo in spending beyond limits and drive the market beyond its capacity to enrich. Credit is a lifetime of angry giving with embossed gold.

We were camped within contiguous clear-cuts that spread to twelve thousand acres at virtually the north-westernmost point of the lower forty-eight. The Bureau of Indian Affairs had the logging rights to this land, owned jointly by local tribes. The Makah, whose revival of the whale hunt was globally protested, ran the Museum at Neah Bay, a cultural attraction for all on our crew. We decided to drive there on our day off. The night before our visit we saw a young man walk out of a bar wearing a red coat with "Makah Nation" in black letters. At the time, I was reading an essay by Peter Berg on nationism in the so-called devolution movement of Europe. This was the early Eighties, and Berg was writing on behalf of Basques, Irish, and Palestinians, whose efforts to devolve are now labeled terrorist. Disestablishing common currency and creating local currencies were among the first steps in devolution. In America, solar communities had begun to devolve, as had people who'd gone off the grid by declaring independence from public utilities, disconnecting from U.S. currency, joining third parties, declaring their own nations. The process could take hundreds of years, though such drastic change may be the goal of sudden uprisings and revolutions. Riots in our streets, however, take place over injustices like WTO, not the theft of a government. Polite enough to wait for the counting of ballots or the verdict of the court, we accepted the coming years, faithful as ever.

We went in one car, about six of us, and drove around Neah Bay for a while before locating the Makah Museum. Near some field, we parked under a telephone wire where three crows perched. That year I finished a long poem based on Northwest native stories collected by anthropologists Boaz and Kroeber. My poem, a simple rendition of interviews with tribal storytellers, proved to me I knew something about Northwest myths, though the dust of education and class hyper-consciousness hadn't washed off in the muddy clear-cut. Since I

137

had practiced my imitation of the Raven's call, I stuck my head out the passenger window, clowning for the backseat, and cawed beseechingly, then looked up. A black eye flicked once, and all three birds shitted on my hat. The experience properly chastened me for our tour of the Makah Museum.

Most of the artifacts under glass came from Ozette Dig, closed due to lack of funding. What the museum preserves far exceeds the expense to maintain the dig. Long walls full of Edward O. Curtis photographs of Makah people led to the whaling exhibit. Only wealthy families could afford the hunt; it may be different now as the tribe attempts to reunite young people in what seems to many a frivolous blood sport. The products of the early hunt were everything manufactured from whale oil, meat, bone, sinew, and gut. The whale was hunted using harpoons made with yew wood shafts, their points of sharpened mussel shell tied to elk antler barbs; these set to oppose the point would fix the harpoon into the whale's side. Stones were tools: whetstones, petroglyphs, and weights, stones for sharpening, carpentry, chisels, and a hammer, adzes, attached by cedar strips. Women made rope from the cedar strips with which, tradition records, the harpooner reeled in his catch. Tools of the builder were made from resources at hand; iron and steel tools drifted the Pacific on Japanese junks borne by the current. The Makah were seafarers whose safety depended on knowledge of weather, and familiarity with the vagaries of climate; designated tribesmen sat on the beach all day observing the color of the sky, wind direction, the sound of water, how vapors rose or lay on hills, the movement of birds, stars, seasons of the moon. Nobody was permitted to talk to them. The Ozette Dig uncovered remnants of a self-sufficient community. Trade and currency were reserved for travelers. Makah weavers made many styles of baskets and an assortment of clothing, woven from cedar bark and the wool of dogs bred for that purpose. Baskets from Eastern Washington tribes were found at the dig, indicating that trade expeditions crossed the Cascades. Salishan, the linguistic family covering the Pacific Northwest, spread and assimilated dialects and cultures. Salishan didn't spread farther east than the Grand Tetons, eliminating contact between the Makah and the Nez Perce, the only Northwest tribe to resist the Europeans. Whites arrived here in smaller numbers than elsewhere. Since trading in sea otter fur, seal skins, whale oil, whalebone, and dentalia was ongoing with tribes to the south and east, as well as Russians, Japanese, Alaskans, and then Europeans, there was no need for tribes in this region to resist. Although they didn't experience "Indian wars," there was still bitterness, the result of broken treaties, the whale hunts only the most publicly decried attempt to restore birthright. Here was a tribe which knew of the treacherous advance of whites, and adopted an ancient approach: trade with the traveler, offer from abundance, give what's lying around, and assimilate. There's so much, who could own it?

My mother on the beach stoops to fill one plastic bag after another with beach glass of all colors, and holds up each to the sun. She keeps them in a special place on a high window sill. She can never use them. She can't go somewhere and hand them over for a loaf of bread or carton of milk. She keeps them for their beauty and abundance, these discards of the sea. California's black market on abalone shells became so inflated that heaps of the shells were hauled away from front yards in coastal towns. A man named Charlie told me he filled his truck at the dump. Traveling east, he spent them on the Hopi reservation for breakfast, groceries, and gasoline. They loved it, and took all he had; he got everything he needed to keep going. Donna polishes common stones. Each takes on such rare qualities that she jars them and locks them in a cabinet when she's away. What dividends could she ever gather from these savings? She always travels with a twenty-dollar bill deep in her purse as a last resort; but the bottom dollar is locked in her polished stones. The eagle feather fastened to a tipi pole stuck out flat and broad as a shelf. I sat there late one night, smoke flying up the smoke hole. One swallow flew in, and alighted quietly beside another; they stayed that way all night. In our tenuous ecological balance, to gather wealth from the land is against the law; national parks and beaches prohibit taking rocks, moss, plants, or disturbing wilderness habitat. Yet climate creates currency. Stones, shells, eagle feathers, woodpecker scalps the Sioux used, are nurtured by ageless climate, the current of air, fire, wind.

I approach a man and woman on stools in a Seattle bar. Near closing time, I'm drunk, almost broke, my unemployment check used up. I know the man, a famous poet, but not the woman. He will not mention her to his wife tomorrow. Taking both in with a sweeping gesture in my oil-stained Army field jacket, I say, "What I really want to know," clumsily yanking my hand out of the jacket pocket, "is why I can't spend this stuff." In that dark city the three of us stare down sadly, resigned to the way things are, at the curled and hollow shapes, a handful of broken shells, shining twisted glass, a smear of white sand along my fingers.

RUNNING ON EMPTY

When we weren't working in the mud, when we weren't covered by it, we were holed up in big green Army tents, smelly like the back of the truck, to dry out, keep warm, cook a little stew for dinner, to make cheese sandwiches without leaving thumb prints, or to lie back and read. Greyhound buses all over town in 1976, the Bicentennial year, history everywhere, the tourist or antique hunter its medium, old rockers, beds, and tables shiny in the storefront windows, a date next to the price—for months we escaped all this to clear-cuts and there we planted trees.

Bob Blair and I shared a tent big enough for cots, boxes of supplies and books, a small round airtight woodstove, and a couple of lamps. Those who'd done this even once before slept in homemade campers mounted on decrepit pickups. We spent a lot of time in woolen long johns, learning more efficient ways to dry clothes. A chaos of lines ranged from the safest point near the stove, clothespins bearing the weight of socks and underwear. We cooked over the woodstove our odd concoctions of carbohydrates and protein; once I gagged a friend with barely cooked grain. Just before first light the mice in our food supply would wake us, we'd stoke the stove, cook some sorry coffee, get back into damp rain gear, and carry soot-stained cheese sandwiches onto the clear-cut, hip bags filled with mud ball treelings, Doug Fir. By now they've probably been harvested by the toilet paper mills.

Some time during those months, Bob and I came up with the idea of publishing a poetry magazine for the Pacific Northwest. Bob had just acquired a Chandler-Price platen press, which he'd installed in a second-floor office of the Taylor Building in Port Townsend. In 1974 many such presses were appearing around town. I helped set type with Bob, Rod Freeman, and Kevin Quigley when they published a collection of poetry and art in 1973 known as *The Wale.* Copies of this book, now rare, were all over Port Townsend and Seattle for about five years. Four or five letterpresses were in the back of the Weir Building, kitty-corner from Seafirst Bank and just across the street from the Town Tavern. The Weir building was unheated, so we spent a great deal of time "planning" at the tavern. The building was being remodeled by Jim Weir, who expressed himself with grunts and gestures. Jim was always framing walls or stairs, then dismantling and reframing. Changing his mind didn't seem unusual, until we came to see the process of assembling and dismantling was chronic, and the building would never be finished.

One of the last flyers printed there was a statement to protest a Kaiser plant in Port Townsend. The day after Kaiser decided not to build, Jim's brother, a millionaire in Seattle, had us kicked out of the building, and those big Chandler-Price printing presses grew feet and walked out. Jim just kept framing, dismantling, and reframing the same vestibule staircase with new beams. He wouldn't look at us. A few years later, a tunnel which originated in the basement of the Weir Building caved in one morning in the middle of Water Street halfway to Seafirst Bank, Jim blinking up into the dust.

Our magazine was going to be printed on one of those letterpress machines, and Bob and I were going survive for a month or so on unemployment checks while hand-setting each page. We had enough material from many fine writers throughout the Northwest to print the first issue of *Dalmo'ma* by Fourth of July, 1976. The title was a Pit River tribal place name I found in Jerry Gorsline's copy of *Indians in Overalls* by the anthropologist Jaime de Angulo. It mattered that the name for the publication should be a place. "Place" for us meant—almost exclusively, and too narrowly—the Olympic Peninsula, but the Pit River people lived in Northern California, beyond the southern boundary of our own region. I had admired the intent of *Kuksu*, a magazine edited by Dale Pendell, Gary Snyder, and Steve Sanfield. What we were doing took some of its influence from their publication, and our title paid homage to stories collected by De Angulo, the French linguist and ethnographer who trained himself to rely on primitive ways. Immediately after the United States incinerated Hiroshima and Nagasaki, he tore a hole in the middle of his living room floor and roof, and heated the home with fire vented through a smoke hole.

The title *Dalmo'ma,* imagined a place such as one in his Pit River songs. It wasn't clear from De Angulo if "Dalmo'ma" was an idealized and imaginary landscape. We were looking for roots we thought we never had, but someone had, and the places we loved contained. Gary Snyder showed up at a reading to benefit one of our early issues and elucidated the etymology of the word "Dalmo'ma," an enlightening linguistic experience to which I hadn't the presence of mind to bring a tape recorder. I remember very little, other than the distinction between glottal stops and glottal clicks. And being forced to admit I knew nothing about the rather odd and apparently meaningless word I'd selected for the title of our magazine, except that I liked what I thought it sounded like in my Euro-tongue's appetite for blithe colonization. I imagined finding, if it were possible, an elder of the Pit River people and asking him, as if I needed to know, what the term might have meant, and being told it was a place of spiritual rebirth, a journey into enlightenment, a vision quest for power, a meeting of the center of one's being with the entire universe. And then I imagined the old man, an old man with long white hair and a lot of wrinkles mapped across his smile, turn away and leave me in hippie reverie at the top of some hill in California, shaking his head and laughing when he got back to his truck and drove away.

But the press name, "Empty Bowl," which fit the Buddhist inclinations of poets who were interested, was Bob

Blair's choice. We set type in that sunny room in the Taylor Building for a few weeks, and printed stacks of several sheets of the little book before I thought to ask the name of the press. I assumed it would be a long process. Bob was setting the chase into the machine to begin our next run. He smoked Drum in those days when we had money, rolling each smoke meticulously so that the end product could have been mistaken for the machined sticks of committed Luckies smokers. Bob was steady and careful in everything he did, and painfully aware of the lack of these qualities in others. Tolerant of my untidiness, however, he pointed out that after typesetting, I always left a pile of small lead type and copper spacers on the workbench, "like a mouse," Bob said, "always a pile of crumbs," and made an unpleasant face.

So now when I thought to introduce the question of the press's name, he stopped locking the chase, and removed the cigarette with its half inch of ash from the corner of his mouth with one hand. Stooping over the work, he turned his face from the press to look at me, and said with one of his maddeningly long pauses, exhaling a cloud of smoke, "Empty Bowl." His look fixing me for a moment more, he put the cigarette back in its place and turned his attention to the machine again.

Although by the second issue, in 1978, Bob was no longer interested in continuing with the project, he put up no resistance when I adopted the Empty Bowl name, as if in a spirit of shared ownership. He said once he'd tried writing poetry and found it easy and didn't want to do it again. Two of his poems are in *Dalmo'ma 1*. He had introduced me to the dark and magical writing of Jorge Luis Borges, and Marcel Duchamp's construction "Bride Stripped Bare by Her Bachelors, Even." But years later, when Bob had an Airstream and traveled as a career reforester, he told me I had "appropriated" the Empty Bowl name and logo when I published *Dalmo'ma 2*. He said so without acrimony, but his choice of words stunned me. My memory of

144

what I had told myself was a transition from dual editorship to collective, diverged widely; yet despite my surprise that he'd seen it so, I could recall no conversation where the name ceased to be his property.

The first time I heard the words "biome" and "bioregions" was when Jerry Gorsline and Linn (now Freeman) House were discussing a scroll entitled "Amble towards Continent Congress" written by Peter Berg. Put out by Planet Drum, this rather formal document presented us for the first time with the idea of a continent divided by natural boundaries. One region begins and another ends where geology and dominant species dramatically change. Trees and flowers, insects, birds, and climate. That places could be structured as natural rather than political systems seemed a more appropriate form of anarchy than measures then being suggested in cities.

Bioregionalism is better explained in the first and second issues of *Dalmo'ma*. In the first issue, Jerry Gorsline's and Linn House's "Excerpts from Future Primitive," and in the second, "Prologue to Ohode R.A.R.E II Proposal" laid out the plan by which bioregionalism accounts for man's place in habitat watershed management. These two pieces of writing constitute the largest portion of prose in the first two issues. They were both scientific as well as poetic solutions to the ancient question, "What is to be done?" The "Prologue" became a centerpiece for the second issue, as did, on the visual level, a set of elegant and symbolic ink drawings by Gué Pilon. The essay was attributed to the collective editorship of Ohode, a group of people on the Olympic Peninsula working "in the realm of watershed politics." For a magazine or anthology to evolve a theme, there must be this conception on the part of the editor that a centerpiece would state the key principles about which all other entries revolved.

The centerpiece of *Dalmo'ma 1* was Mike O'Connor's "Song of Ishi," a poem cycle derived from *Ishi: in Two Worlds* by Theodora Kroeber. The poems include some in Chinook jargon, which, as every Washington State history student learns, is the language created specifically for trade among whites and natives of the Pacific Northwest. Throughout the book, Puget Sound Salishan calendar terms set the poems and translations in specific seasonal turns. There were Aztec and Sioux translations within these few pages and in both the first and second issues the poetry and stories of such writers as Tim McNulty, William Stafford, Kim Stafford, Bill Ransom, Sam Hamill, Barry Lopez, Jim Dodge, John Haines, and Jim Heynen.

Both issues quickly sold out at $2 each, and Empty Bowl's loose-knit group of editors and friends fell back into meetings, reading, and discussion. The press was occasionally busy. Two issues of a pamphlet series, *Firecrackers*, went out, and a few small postcard-size poems. *Firecrackers 2* was produced by D. J. Hamilton and consisted of his translation from the Spanish text of a poem by the Palestinian, Mahmud Darweesh. It included a rough map of the strife-torn Middle East, about which most of us entrenched regionalists knew utterly nothing. *Firecrackers 1*, which I edited, consisted of three poems by Tim McNulty, Tom Jay, and Doug Dobyns. The subtitle, "Poems against Trident," marked the first occasion for Empty Bowl to speak against the Navy's proposed submarine base a few miles from where we lived. *The Pacific Northwest Review of Books* noted the special paper was like brown bag. It may be the "prime directive" of regionalism that artists work with local materials. Like prehistoric regionalists in Jim Dodge's Lascaux ("Magic and Beauty" *Dalmo'ma 2*), we found that Empty Bowl could, as if magically, attract what was needed from the community. A roll of brown paper from the Port Townsend mill which employed most of the town and fouled the air with pulp fumes, appeared at the door. We could work it on the letterpress if it was cut. The three-foot roll became an insurmountable problem for days until someone came by the office with a chainsaw, divided it into three neat rolls, and left. On a small green paper cutter from the local thrift store, I unrolled the brown bag material and sliced nearly precise sheets into two stacks I flattened with the OED.

146

Composed mainly of people fresh from what we saw as victory in the pullout from Vietnam, activists protested the production and proliferation of the Trident Nuclear Submarine System, and production and shipment of weapons-grade material. Though the three or four white-haired men and women standing in front of thousands of municipal locations across the country today continue to be a more emphatic pronouncement against military build-up, the obligation to provide witness to warmongers and governments is the lasting purpose of such struggles. Empty Bowl began the first *Dalmo'ma Anthology* by publishing, collecting, and disseminating significant documents of the Northwest anti-Trident movement.

The book includes a statement by spokesperson Jim Douglass, as well as the "Defendants' Trial Brief on International Law," which declared the Trident illegal on grounds it is a first-strike weapon. Jerry Gorsline published an interview with a young Buddhist monk who along with a small group from Japan built a temple on Ground Zero. On a day when our tree-planting crew helped with construction, we met Archbishop Hunthausen, who attended protests against Trident, called it the "New Auschwitz," and withheld his taxes. When they had completed the temple, built on property adjoining the Bangor Naval Base, Trident's home port, it was burnt to the ground by unknown arsonists. Jim Douglass used the term *satyagraha*, in his essay on peace in this anthology; he translates the Hindu as "truth-force," which accurately depicted the modesty and respect with which private citizens confronted this inhumanly aggressive machine.

To the anti-Trident section, the anthology linked Central American poetry and essays, and the work of writers about the environment, feminism, and Northwest poetry, specifically. Sharon Doubiago's wilting depiction of male writers in the "Bearshit in the Trail School of Poetry" indicted many poets who had been models for our publications. Although her essay took its initial outrage from the second issue's call for submissions on the theme, "Balling The Great Mother," she wrote persuasively

147

about the lack of representation by women in a movement that took language about earth from maternal images. While producing the first issue of *Dalmo'ma,* I had attended Kenneth Rexroth's workshop at Centrum's first summer writing program. He had a great deal to say about publishing, as well as about writing and influences beginning writers could best profit from. Rexroth said without sarcasm that editors who start poetry magazines do so to publish their own poetry. I had to admit this was true, though Bob and I were committed to the work of authors we'd invited. That was 1976. By 1982, our anthology's commitment was to issues, thoughtful arguments, compelling images, and serious alternatives. One reviewer chastised our representing too many controversies. In hindsight her criticism is justified, yet we found it ludicrous. How could we not combine themes? Each depends on the other. As a group of editors meeting in one another's living rooms, we could not criticize the government without looking at the governed. We examined aggression in its pertinent forms. Yet we wanted our anthology to express hope. For that we selected from among the elegant photographs of Steven R. Johnson, and reproduced a triptych of paintings in black-and-white by the late Northwest artist, Nelson Capouilliez. The struggles and compromises of a collective editorship of eleven people forced us to balance our interests with the central theme, a life at peace, or as bumper stickers were saying, "Live Without Trident." Our belief in the value of individuals and communities standing up at forums not only to protest higher property taxes governed our efforts to publish.

Our struggle to combine a variety of themes fostered disagreement about what a Northwest poet was. A regional writer is not necessarily provincial but can one ask such a question without also asking what is a New York Poet, or a San Francisco, Los Angeles, Latino, or Chicago poet. "What is a regional poet?" settles nothing about the Northwest or any location. except to identify an address or influence. The Northwest suggests movie settings, coffee companies, mountains and rivers, logging. Since software often originates here, a Northwest poet might write exclusively for cyber readerships, where a poet's sensory observations need have no definable influence. It seems that a writer who has not been somewhat formed by a specific place can't really be called "regional," and that his or her references to place are backdrop and props. Empty Bowl was profoundly committed to one place; were we deceived into thinking that Northwest native Gary Snyder was a Northwest poet? Was he a California poet because he lived in the Sierras, and wrote about his community's claim on that place? Was Robinson Jeffers a California poet? Lawrence Ferlinghetti a San Francisco poet? And Rexroth? Was Robert Frost a New England poet? The answer of course is always "Yes," in the same way that Shakespeare was an English playwright. Yet, he is "the Bard," and they are "poets," our models who gained national audiences. Terms like Northwest, local, or regional for a poet may be pejorative, belittling someone who refuses to publish with the multinationals. A Northwest poet, with or without corporate readerships, writes what interests people from the Northwest.

When we finished the *Dalmo'ma Anthology* we felt we were not a "literary" magazine. (We still thought we would produce an issue more than once a year, but soon gave that up, and referred to subsequent volumes as the *Dalmo'ma* series.) We meant to be more useful than strictly literary, prejudiced in favor of the broadest interpretations, yet I think the *Dalmo'ma Anthologies* remain as literary text in their representation of the pastoral tradition. Just as Stephen Duck, who protested the advent of the Industrial Revolution with proletariat poetry predating Marxism, and John Clare of the same era who with mad ferocity describes down to the nose hairs every badger in sight, Empty Bowl and centuries of local poets have found a sacred grove. Robert Frost and Virgil meditated on how the human condition thrives in the vegetative bucolic, and Gary Snyder depicted the ghost logger visiting the demolished grove.

Our *Dalmo'ma's* sought wilderness treasured by those who could not live in imaginary landscapes.

When Empty Bowl became a nonprofit organization, I was officially hired as editor-publisher trainee. An out-of-work tree planter rehabilitating from an injured back, I was eligible for retraining funded by the Washington State Department of Labor and Industries for six months. Although our organization had to agree to hire me at the end of that period, we knew the chances were slim that Empty Bowl could afford an employee. It seems now to have been a shady deal, but even the tree planters who disapproved of my L & I claim thought support of the press a community obligation.

Digging for Roots: Dalmo'ma 5, edited by Christina Pacosz and Susan Oliver in l984, contained "Works by Women of The North Olympic Peninsula" and was funded by anonymous donations. In 1986 we published two issues funded by a grant from the Washington State Arts Commission's dwindling arts fund. Edited by Finn Wilcox and Jerry Gorsline, *Working The Woods Working The Sea, Dalmo'ma VI: An Anthology of Northwest Writings.* I edited *Dalmo'ma 7: In Our Hearts & Minds, The Northwest & Central America. Working the Woods,* perhaps the only book to portray the lives and experiences of tree planters, examines the neglect of watershed management, the status of the Pacific Northwest as a resource colony for timber and fish, the losses of variety species in plant, fish, and animals. Its attitude toward environment is captured best in two essays at the end of the book, "Twana Fjord" by Jerry Gorsline and "Salmon of the Heart" by Tom Jay. *In Our Hearts & Minds* is a collection of writing by Central Americans and Northwesterners regarding tragedies in El Salvador, Nicaragua, Guatemala, and Honduras. Expanding our sense of community, it demonstrated accomplishments of the Sister Cities, and established a relationship with environmental issues beyond our bioregion. With these three books we focused on the major themes our first reviewer had faulted us for treating like buckshot.

The last issue in the series was published in 1992 and called *Shadows of Our Ancestors, Dalmo'maVIII: Readings in the History of Klallam-White Relations,* . Edited with commentaries by Jerry Gorsline, it is monumental in the scope of Empty Bowl's vision. The collection addresses eloquently and precisely the themes fundamental to our publications: regional, environmental, native, and historic values override the general, vague, inexact blunders of political and academic systems. The book's copyright page makes this final declaration of our identity: "Empty Bowl is a small, non-profit press dedicated to publishing books and periodicals that reflect the visions and concerns of Pacific Rim communities, biological and cultural features of distinct regions, and the interdependence of all life along the Pacific Rim. *The Dalmo'ma Anthology* is an ongoing publication program interpreting Pacific Rim culture, history, and ecology."

Our emphasis on the Pacific Rim included books by Bill Porter (Red Pine) and Mike O'Connor, sent from Taiwan. *The Rainshadow* (1983), our first book published in Taiwan and bound in the traditional Chinese fashion, included O'Connor's poems about China with those set near the eastern slope of the Olympics. Red Pine sent beautiful exotic copies of *P'u Ming's Oxherding Pictures & Verses* (1983), *From Temple Walls: The Collected Poems of Big Shield and Pickup* (1984), *The Mountain Poems of Stonehouse* (1986), and the first English translation of *The Zen Teaching Of Bodhidharma* (1987), the Buddhist patriarch, all translated into modern English and bearing our logo, the half circle of the bowl.

Apart from the *Dalmo'ma* series, we'd begun to publish individual collections of poetry. Funding was always up to the author for these books. Although all such publications can be tarred as vanity or subsidy books, we were not inviting authors to submit based on their bank accounts, or their benefactors', but because their work was significant to many of us in the editorial committee, because the work struck us as powerful interpretations of our human involvement with this region.

Non-profit presses are the staple of a strong regional literature, without which the literature from any area is left to the press attracting the most grants. Grant support depends on past performance, which means bigger more beautiful books by more celebrated authors. More and more, as funding from government and foundations channels toward the largest, most competitive small presses, and as "reader fees" increase disproportionately to the price of books, poets actively pursue funding, give up the long-awaited approval of some venerable editor, and sometimes pony up the cost themselves. A misfortune of such developments is the diminished role of editors in subsidy presses. Compared to those graduate students or hired guns who pre-read contest submissions, one's friends are less reliable; yet a negative response by impartial readers genuinely moved by poetry can be as rewarding as acceptance into the world of academic look-alikes. Unsure of our worth in the competitive market, we approached writing with astonishing authority. Who, after all, was Dante's editor? Whitman's? Rilke's? Yeats'? Certainly Pound reading Yeats' later poems had an influence, as he did on Eliot and many other poets of his day. Who edited Pound?

Finn Wilcox's *Here Among the Sacrificed* is a collection of haunting poems and captivating stories about his travels on freight trains, accompanied by startling and beautiful photos by Steven R. Johnson. American hobos, Finn said, were their own bioregion. While we were in the midst of publication, I returned to the

East Coast to help my family. (At least three of our six editors, Northwest writers, came from New England.) I was living alone in a small cottage on Martha's Vineyard for a few weeks, where I cut and pasted with a chalky ruler on the kitchen table. Most book designers are more rigid. I rented a light table from a typesetter and tried to keep my lines straight. Steve Johnson and I were on the phone every day discussing placement of photos or quality of printing.

Finn Wilcox, Pat Fitzgerald, and Jerry Gorsline ran Empty Bowl for fourteen years, disbanding the nonprofit and dispersing unsold books in 1998. They were filling orders, though fewer and fewer, years after books were published. Despite minimal advertisement, few reviews, and increasing disillusionment, orders came steadily from book stores, distributors, collectors and readers of poetry and literature throughout the world. They published *Working the Woods Working the Sea* (1986), *Shadows of Our Ancestors* (1992) and *Psyche Drives the Coast* (1990) by Sharon Doubiago. They facilitated the distribution of Empty Bowl books produced by associates of the press, such as *Whole Houses Shaking* (1993) by Jim Bodeen, *The Family Letters of Maxwell Perkins* (1995) , edited by Jerry Gorsline, and *Untold Stories* (1990) by William Slaughter. They placed many of our books in classrooms as texts for college and high school courses.

Migrating from Bob Blair's office to Nelson Capouilliez' vacant garage, to various pickup trucks, once to a closet behind a bakery, twice to spacious unheated offices overlooking the downtown traffic of tourists and poets, and often to kitchens and tables of our fluctuating membership for board meetings or mailings, to plan auctions and fundraisers or rock concerts, to design books and edit, Empty Bowl was a moveable feast; and the party wound up in Pat and Finn's living room. They stored books for years in their house and their kids grew up with poets and readers coming and going to pick up or autograph copies. They ran meetings and kept accounts of an organization whose name meant replenishment, the gift that moves. They saw the spontaneity of poetry needed to come to rest somewhere, and they took on the steady methodical job, permitting writers and artists a home. The press kept a place for writers to publish works significant to Northwest literature. The more nebulous and loose, the more apparent became Empty Bowl's purpose: to record an era in regional literary history and represent the tradition of those who stand apart. From our home, and with local materials, we did what literature commands: we made a solid thing of words.

In August, 2006, Empty Bowl was reborn under the direction of Mike O'Connor with the publication of The Blossoms are Ghosts at the Wedding: Selected Poems and Essays, *by Tom Jay*

IV

I left Portland on nothing but a breeze.
Afraid of jets, having lost my faith in air, I stood
in a boxcar door, heading up Columbia Gorge,
late moony light splintering the floor.
My hands were rocks in a big green coat.
Laddie rode the trains because he crashed a truck,
the farmer's milk beside the white chickens.
Story coupled to story,
rattling through a tunnel and back out,
he talked through the clash of steel and echo,
no one following, his white beard floating the tilt of moon.
In moon a girl raised her hand as we were passing the garden,
and waved her baby's hand, a rapid pulse along my throat.
"There is a ship," he tells me, "travels across space
playing Louis Armstrong for fifty years on a gold record.
I want to be there, but where is space?
Where is it?" Fingers curve the air.
A year later I found him in the Market
with a cup out, singing little Polish tunes,
shoppers drifting past us. Small dried flowers,
purple and white, blew out of his pocket.
1931, the first night in the pit of a boxcar,
Milwaukee already asleep in his father's pasture,
he cried for knit pillow feathers from geese he'd plucked.
They can make a footprint for a hundred windless years.
He squeezes his fists, smooths some ground
for a "jug all day under the peach orchards,"
and into my pocket pours his cup of quarters.

OF APHRODITE'S
DEATHLESS SMILE

There is no life

that couldn't be immortal

if only for a moment

——*Wislawa Szymborska*

*"Brother," said the man in Athens hardly trying to sell us gold
and silver, "what do you think about so much?" Like a Zen koan from
Zorba, his question woke me up: why so preoccupied with dumb fate?
Here of all places I should not think so much, caught again on vacation
with my heart's jazzy beat, atrial fibrillation again leading me to
hospitals in foreign countries, EKGs and injections. I spent three hours
in the Evangelist Hospital Emergency Room, waiting for my heart to
defibrillate in a hallway packed with trauma— families in turmoil, a
woman moaning, another wailing in anguish, others holding smashed
or broken noses; the catheter bottle one man elevates with both hands
leashes his friend shuffling past, tube in arm; some squeezed tight the
coats of little wives or daughters skeptical about their own illnesses;
some with worry beads in one hand, cell phone in the other, the same
annoying tune every few minutes, in business suits and silver beads—
elegant, commanding, fully in charge even in the face of the nothing
medicine can do now; and an ambulance driver scatters the crowd pushing
the gurney, another driver pressing rapidly a little gray-haired man's
heart, a half-filled beach ball, in purple pajama shirt fluttering up
and out. The man's brother, by family resemblance, kept close watch at
the Kardiologia's swinging doors, distress and pain in his face. After a
half hour two younger people enter there with him—a man in a bright
blue shirt and a woman already in black. She and the brother emerge*

after a while. She is convulsed in tears, the brother attempting to quiet her. In a little while they all leave, the brother tapping the man in the blue shirt on the shoulder, telling him how to help with the woman's grief. Younger than the deceased, he has always helped and will not show his grief or wonder who will grieve when undoubtedly in the not-too-distant future he is wheeled here, too. Soon they brought the dead man out; although a white sheet was over his face, I could tell by the length of its corpse and his shabby gray hair who he was.

Apollo is the name of the ferry we're taking back to Athens and also the name of our hotel on the day after the streets of Paros were flooded—a real gully-washer, one of those obscure words I've made some of my classes learn. The streets were flowing with a strong current, so brown it must have carried topsoil from the rocky hillsides. Mr. Kyriakos told us in his wife's impeccable living room that they have been having excellent weather, and we would enjoy our stay in the villa we rented from him. There has been no rain for two years. "A drought," I said, though he seemed unfamiliar with this word. I mentioned that where we live rain never stops, but he seemed unimpressed. It must have been difficult to grow anything on this island. Yet the place has plenty of orchards, grape arbors, and olive trees. Crops have been hurt, he tells me. Flowers I can't name ornament the white stone and plaster walls; pink, vermillion, and blue, they droop from vines to walkways of villas high in the hills overlooking Paros's harbor where the morning ferry was the main show. Their scent is for us drifters exotic perfume. When we called it "villa," we exaggerated a little our importance—the naiveté and arrogance of Westerners; called "pigeon towers," slate cubicles built into the walls allowed the roosting and laying of eggs. Hillsides supply builders with walls and fences like New England's which make such good neighbors but here discourage goats from roaming and support the terraced hills.

158

We left the villa scribbling a note in what I thought close to Greek, to Kyriakos, Anna, and their daughter, Aristea. Yesterday we were on the streets in the torrent; our clothes at the laundromat dried as those we wore got drenched, but our coats, shoes, and pants needed more time in the drier, shoes a day and a night beside an oven. The slightly obnoxious ticket sellers at the ferry office (Charon's staff) acted put out that I wanted to know the latest schedule. "Ask me again at 6," said a smug man barely raising his eyes from the computer. Maybe it was my look of dumb shock that the ferry would not run all day. After days on beaches around Paros, sudden rain was not enough to convince me drastic weather approached. At the Apollo I saw the TV broadcast the island had been watching for days. A severe snowstorm in northern Greece, crippling winds on the high seas, belted the Aegean, Athens, and all the Cyclades. No, they didn't know when the next ferry would leave—"Of course not— maybe Sunday, maybe Monday, probably Tuesday."

The Apollo is a B class hotel; a sign along the beach advertises as much. 7,000 drachmas, a good deal. We told the woman at the desk that Stefanos the car rental man told us his mother— "Are you his mother?"—would rent a room at that price; she looked stricken, perhaps, I thought, because she doesn't speak English. I've seen the look often now. An older person wants to answer my idiotic questions—often asked to pass the time. I forget how much it takes. But with her it was different. She said something in Greek, and we smiled foolishly. Then she held up an index finger, gave a slight smile and went into another room. She returned with a young woman, a daughter. "Can I help you?" I was surprised that someone who spoke English so fluently lived on the island year-round. She must have gone away to college and returned here to the family business. She let us know this was not Stefanos's mother, but his mother-in-law, a fine distinction, but important to the woman, Eleni, in the black dress whispering something to her daughter, her forehead furrowed more than when we entered the lobby. "9,000 drachmas, not 7," said the daughter. It was the effort to communicate the price without scaring us or casting aspersions on Stefanos that had troubled her.

The dining room was decorated with red velvet curtains, tall, high-back chairs, velvet-covered tables with turned oak legs, and life-size statues, likenesses of classical sculpture. The two I recognized were "The Sea's Daughter" and "David." Similar statues of deities, perfect white figures startling against velvet curtains, stood throughout the lobby and beside stairs leading to bigger rooms than ours on the first floor with bath and bidet (which crowded the bathroom so you couldn't stand at the sink, but sat on the large tub to brush your teeth). All in all, Apollo was a tad pretentious. The business cards bore the name, Theo Yanaros, and the slogan: "The place to see. The place to be seen." Apart from my interest in his first name, the same as my son's, the name struck me because no male exuded proprietary airs as manager, owner, husband, or Zeus-like paterfamilias; nor were there Apollos at the Apollo. In fact, no music, no art other than the forlorn statues awaiting spring light, curtains awaiting breezes recalled by Aeolus. We were low-season patrons, bottom fish, dregs, arrived when prices sank, beaches emptied. On the ferry dock four young men and a middle-aged woman asked if we needed a good hotel, each with a concerned look I've learned to avoid answering skeptically. It was the expression of a child watching a helium balloon vanish in the sun; three lone travelers arriving in Paros meant the inflated drachma floats higher out of reach. Later Stefanos' wife would show an almost indifferent air toward our money; any price would do, whenever we paid—now, later, not at all—it was all the same. I came upon this brand of generosity on our last day, returning to pay for a long-distance call I'd made earlier. I received an amused smile as if I needn't have done that. A recognition that the inflated economy produces laughable efforts in tourists who fork over a pittance to feel honest. The tip I offered our waiter one morning after breakfast he flatly refused; after such an inexpensive meal, I could not have left enough small change to make accepting it worthwhile. Perhaps he wanted me to save face. Eleni refused to accept more money from us the morning we left Apollo, but for different reasons: it was unfair to pay after such a night.

She didn't just follow good practices of the hospitality industry. Nor did Anna Kyriakos when she came across her tiled patio, leaving clothesline and laundry, to greet Kathy and me warmly with a firm handshake and bright smile, and when she invited us into her house where thirteen-year-old Aristea, whose English was very good, sat at a table spread like a feast. Anna fed us, gave us wines and dessert, coffee and ouzo, obeying ancient Greek law. It's what got Odysseus in so much trouble. He got off on the wrong foot with Polyphemus pointing out that the Cyclops showed no proper hospitality when he discovered Odysseus and crew plundered victuals they uncovered in nooks and crannies of his cave. Strangers are sent by the gods, *Theoi*. Achaean custom demanded guests, strangers, friends, and visitors be treated as gods. Which irritated Polyphemus who blasted the wanderer with a resounding disparagement of the Pantheon, despite he was Poseidon's son, nephew to Zeus, and promptly gobbled up several of the crew. The gods didn't like the inhospitable. A useful custom to mention while raping and pillaging, an Achaean past-time as flotillas slipped away from the rubble of Troy. To look upon the hero from Ithaca as a kind of Ur-tourist seems degrading, though kindness in their industry is completely genuine. What prompted my distrust when an Athenian taxi driver offered two hotels, good family places three times the price of our hostel, was a sense the vanquished assimilate those who conquer, even by exchange rate, by enticing the stereotype: nice family rooms, "the place to be seen," life-size gods to fill a cave with kitsch. If Polyphemus had only known.

Eleni's Theo may have died and these business cards I came across, when everything was up for grabs, may have been outdated.

161

Perhaps she never thought of the Apollo as anything but his, which explains her traditional black dress. It's hard to say how much was hers. The classical tone, the ornamental bar, the beautiful wood floor, oriental rugs, and furniture may have been purchased by them both, though I suspect she would not have chosen naked naiads and voluptuous goddesses to welcome guests. Eleni seemed not to notice the statues among details which determined our relationship—towels, blankets, French doors onto the low balcony a few feet above an extensive brick patio which wandered the various buildings and led uphill where evening's drizzle stippled the river current. She operated her husband's hotel as sole executor with a sharp eye on waste at this end of the season, setting a value on the generosity she could afford; she would have charged us to turn on the heat, but while we were out to dinner brought extra blankets and remade the beds, a kindness we hadn't expected

In the unlit dining room, the round oak tables covered in velvet and white linen and set with empty crystal bowls, napkins, salt and pepper, an old woman sat in an easy chair in front of a big screen TV. For a while, a little girl was playing with some Legos and a doll. Once I noticed the old woman had fallen asleep, her white hair tied in a bun, black shawl round her shoulders; another time she looked up and smiled beatifically. She reminded me of Marquez's Ursala in *A Hundred Years of Solitude* who had gotten so small in old age she had shriveled like a raisin and her great grandchildren treated her as a toy. I wondered if she remembered the horrors of civil war, less than fifty years ago? Or the Fascist military regimes, or knew of the centuries of conquest that formed modern Greece? Did she know of the contemporary artists in the Cyclades steeping themselves in ancient models? Mostly men, they'd created replicas out of Paros marble of figures currently on display in an Athens museum. The City in a City exhibit. Paros marble lets light shine in the stone. A style of sculpture emerged which offered a stark sexless figure, the tip of whose nose rises above the surface of each moon-shaped face, hapless as mimes. The antithesis of ancient Athens replicated in the tall ceramics throughout the Apollo, these have no expression, no articulated gesturing limbs, heroic and divine, no theatrical poses. Cycladic sculpture pointedly represses such features, offers instead blind white marble posed as the equivalent of stick figure drawings. This too is us, they say. So does Eleni's mother's blissful smile, and this fringe of the birthplace of culture, islands once victims of the boot, the submachine gun, and history's wheel.

These artists I imagine were not so different from men I met in Greece. Flamboyant, yet kind and thoughtful, they walk the sunny streets; or gruff and dour, they are intent on an enterprise and as thorough and detached as Mafia dons lest their families and businesses perish. Yet each fingers his worry beads, a custom that concentrates on the success of the moment— business, friendship, or both—a thread never to release, and never fear showing how sincerely they hold to integrity. Not only the birthplace of macho, the male identity with the heroic, Greece of course invented Western Civilization, as well as *Gaia*, from this feminine landscape where hills, draped in light reflected in white marble and plaster walls, slope toward a shining sea. Under the full moon are tinted orchards and arbors and narrow cobbled streets and cafés; from here came that name for earth which now depicts a genderless object of the scientific mind, not to mention the economic and geopolitical scorned metaphor of the earth mother, or the challenge of 21st century man who scales the rocky slope because it's there, not because it's sacred.

After Eleni in black dress and slight smile gave us towels and key, and later water and *Metaxa*, which I sipped to console myself over missing our ferry, we got comfortable in the room, my lucky number seven, ate the sandwiches we'd prepared for the long ferry ride back to Athens, and watched until too late the intricate and innovative ballet of Jackie Chan against insipid and unsuspecting TV bad guys. It may be a long time before popular culture comes 'round again to the expression of heroism and indomitable will found on sculpted faces of Athens and blank ones of the Cyclades. At any rate, we could go to sleep, and hope that tomorrow another ferry might run despite predictions of the worst. A light rain fell on the balcony outside the glass doors.

*

In the dark under two soft blue blankets, I hear my son in the bathroom. He's eleven and to think of him getting up in the middle of the night like the old man worries me, especially since he's taking so long and why doesn't he have the light on? Moonlight out the French doors. How loud the rain is. Maybe something's wrong. Nosebleeds come for no reason in the middle of the night. It's like velvet running over your lip, he says; but I should get up anyway because the neon clock face says it's exactly 2.30 in the AM and I could see if he was up at 5 or 6 but this has me worried, and even though I was having a good dream I'd better be getting back to, I should see what the problem is, and right away as soon as I put my foot down I see I left the latch undone again on a window, or the French doors because oh-my-god there's a stream of water and my son's in his bed and the water course is rushing in through open doors over the balcony where it's raining so hard, so very hard, and the trickle has reached the entry to the bathroom and the light switch as soon as I reach it I worry will electrify this rainwater now up to my toes the poor carpet already spongy. There's a woman wailing out in the lobby. I hear her over a loud current rushing up my ankles. Kathy is by now awake and Teddy too because I've been swearing in the dark. "Oh, no, did you leave a window open again?" "No, no, I don't think so, it wasn't me," as I lean out of the doorway and peer down the hall, bracing the door against the force of water five inches up my leg. The lobby light is on, white statues waving silly hands, wild screaming and white water rushing through the lobby and down the front stairs.

"Come on. We've got to leave," I tell Kathy and Teddy and begin throwing things into open bags. "Take everything that's important," I say. "Here are your pants. Here are your shoes. Put them in a bag. Come on. Come on. Let's go." And they look at me, blinking from the beds; half smiling like this is some goofy way to cover for having left the window open. "Hurry up," I say. "Okay, okay," like they're going back to sleep for a few more minutes, and I keep packing things into black bags. We didn't bring much, most of it still packed, so it's not that hard, but I can't remember where the switch is for the lights to this room, and water is up to my knees, the woman screaming out there like a mother on the plain of battle. I'm sure it's Eleni.

I move between luggage and closet. I have gotten dressed in shorts and a fleece vest, packed my shoes, dry after yesterday's torrent in the streets of Paros, and as I lumber past the short floating refrigerator, I get an electrical shock up my legs. Now I'm scared. The door has shut and we can't go over the low balcony. Kathy and Teddy reluctantly get on some clothes. I have a vision of us trapped, standing on beds to avoid electrocution. "We're being evacuated," I tell them. "We have to move out now! Let's go!" I'm not sure whether we will be evacuated. I imagine boats in the streets, helicopters plucking us off the roof. I imagine the streets flooded and wish we had stayed up at the villa. But they respond pretty well to that word "evacuated," and we each carry a pack or bag, hold our shoes up in the air and carefully high-step past the fridge. Then we work our way through the hall, forcing the door back open—a tall man splashes down the hall and says with an Aussie accent, " 'Avin' fun now, 'ey?" The water over our knees, we step delicately barefoot down the corridor, the current pouring across the lobby, Eleni's voice not the inarticulate grieving I'd heard but a steady stream of Greek wail at someone on the other end of her cell, three other men, apparently boarders, stand on about the fourth stair, the carpet on the first already soaked.

One of the difficulties of being understood in a language with which you're barely familiar is that every sound you emit communicates. No utterance escapes the responsibility to bear meaning. How easily we forget, we "ugly Americans" who insist one language is enough but blunder into another to learn the prices of items we're adding to our accumulated travel memorabilia or the whereabouts of sanitary water closets. I don't often recognize that saying anything on certain occasions, in any language, is useless, but I did then, before them on the stairs, their puzzled calm gazes cast at the water rushing past our knees and over the vestibule stairs. Eleni on the phone looked at me for one moment and stopped her screaming long enough to remember we were those guests of one or two nights in Room 7 who spoke not a word of Demotic Greek. Her gesture the instant she resumed her tirade to her daughter or son on the other end of the phone, or maybe an emergency officer who should come and save us all, indicated we should step out of the water and onto the stairs near the three little men crowded like Greek pigeons on a float log. Her eyes swept past us and fell back instantly to the water level rising near the top of the entry door, her hand snapping toward us with perfunctory grace.

The entry to the Apollo was up a flight of stairs, and this entire stairwell was filled by the rushing stream of water crossing her carpet. Water up the glass doors and windows which faced the street, I could see nothing outside, but assumed that another wall of water pressed against the outside of the doors. But in only a few minutes a jeep pulled up and its headlights revealed no more than a foot of water rushing down the street; our danger was not the tide rising, but the flood in the lobby dammed by the locked front doors. As the jeep smashed the glass of one front door, Eleni screamed even more hysterically. No vehicle tonight could get up the speed to impact the glass enough, and no one could (especially not me tempted as always to) swim down there, open the locked doors from the inside and let all the water out (save the island and gain the undying gratitude of both modern Greeks and ancient Achaeans) because whoever tried it (I, the hero) would be swept out onto the street by the force of water and (martyred and celebrated in song and legend) crack his skull open on the threshold (memorial stone erected with picture, flowers changed twice weekly).

A man outside the glass door holding a flashlight in one hand, a hammer in the other, tapped the glass out of two small panes below the water, and the flood drained onto the street. She screamed furiously, but he kept doing it. She screamed when he reached through a broken pane, unlocked the glass doors and let rushing water flood the street exposing stairs, oriental rug, and the lobby floor covered, as we saw eventually, in shallow puddles formed by mud three inches thick over the carpet, the beautiful floor, chair legs, mud plugging shut the bottoms of doors, filling the rooms down the hall where neat, well-made beds, blankets, and towels awaited just such a disturbance or the first daring off-season guests to stride eagerly over the carpet now wrinkled into waves like tidal sand, all her beautiful and uninsured rugs, all of it, all of it, turned to river mud.

We worked all night with brooms, and squeegees to clear mud and silt off Eleni's beautiful floors. Kathy found a room for Teddy upstairs, and he went back to sleep, then both of us helped with the endless cleanup. Upstairs in the hall, she met Eleni's mother sitting on a stiff-backed chair rescued from the dining room, talking with men who took a break from sweeping to have a smoke. She told me I had dirty feet; one of the men translated. Kathy learned she was cold and offered her warm brown fleece. So the grandmother sat in the stiff chair all night wrapped in my wife's comfortable coat. While we and the sons and daughter, nephews, nieces, and neighbors tried to save the dining room,

167

Eleni wailed in the kitchen, giving commands and complaining. In Rooms 7 and 9 and 14 and along the hall, keening every few minutes enough to shatter the silence most of us maintained while we swept. Or at least which Kathy and I maintained while sweeping with the Greeks, their language passing over and through us sometimes beautifully, sometimes harshly in rhythms of steady work, but more often in a panic to remove mud, or outraged at one another for doing it all wrong. We worked all night with them. It was some of the best hours we'd spent in months, doing work for a good purpose. Kathy became concerned about Eleni and asked her daughter if their mother would be okay. "Oh, yes, she's all right. She's . . . a little bit crazy right now, but she will be all right. She's complaining because a bridge was never repaired up the hill behind us, and the river has broken through. Why doesn't the city pay for this damage, she wants to know?" Indeed, later in the night Eleni was in the street lambasting, or directing like a general in battle, city workers and firemen who brought a generator and were pumping water off her property. She was marching back and forth outside in a black raincoat, rubber boots, and pink hair curlers.

Around five in the morning the daughter told us, as designated spokeswoman, that they were grateful for our help, but we should rest now. She would find us towels and blankets and we could use the room where our son was sleeping. As we left the dining room, one son washed down our feet and legs with the garden hose he had brought in to rinse the silt off everything. While he sprayed down the David statue, everyone laughed hysterically; he was cleaning mud off David's testicles. It was the first time I'd heard anyone laugh that night. Meanwhile Eleni in a distant room rattled off some new tirade.

Next morning we returned from breakfast and learned the ferry would be leaving soon. Eleni entered from the hall, her look like that of a startled animal; eyes gauging the use of compassion, she nodded and kept going. Later, saying goodbye in the lobby, we wanted to pay what we owed, but she wouldn't hear of it. She was grateful, the daughter translated, and we should not think of paying. Then Kathy remembered the brown fleece she'd loaned to the grandmother. The daughter told Eleni. After they looked around the lobby and couldn't find it, they went upstairs to find grandmother asleep under a big quilt, wearing the brown fleece. Eleni, Kathy and Eleni's daughter stood at the foot of the bed looking at the sleeping woman, long gray hair spread over the pillow like a fan. She would not open her eyes, but smiled from a dream, while Eleni and her daughter carefully removed one arm then the other from the fleece. With an almost imperceptible smile herself, Eleni turned to Kathy, and the three of them started to laugh, but stopped after only a moment.

HUNGARIAN NOTEBOOK

Today we rode the bikes we bought last fall, before ice and snow, the worst winter Hungary had seen in twenty years. On icy mornings my son and I waited at the tram stop, frozen for the ten minutes it took the next tram to squeal around the corner near our street, an icebox crammed with children and gabby women from the open market, warming one another with thin smiles. But now it's spring, and we get to ride bikes again. Some Hungarians biked in the snow, but I wanted to avoid another stay in the hospital. The bikes still new, mine a beautiful, bright blue, Teddy's silver and shiny black. As my bad pronunciation does, so do these bikes set us apart as wealthy Americans. We rode to Szecenyi Ter, the park in the center of town—sycamore-lined lawns, statues from pre-Communism. Crossing tram tracks near the Posta, an imposing edifice where citizens wait in long lines to collect letters and packages or pay utility bills, I thought I saw Kovacs Peter and circled near the tram stop where he stood. I didn't want to stare, but the man had his distinctive hooked nose, thin slicked-back white hair. His black suit, though open at the throat, was more formal than was Peter's style—then again I'd only seen him in pajamas, and it had been all the long winter since our encounter. Slowing the bike as I approached, I realized my mistake; this was a different Hungarian, also carrying the 20th century on his back.

Twice since, I've seen him in windows of passing trams, and the second time he didn't look well. Weeks after my stay at the Klinika, my doctor told me Peter was no longer a patient. He'd been there for a gastrointestinal disorder, the chief health problem among men, stomach cancer leading the causes of

170

death. Not that I worried. As an Angol Lector (English conversation teacher), I was more concerned with the future of Hungary, a term I meant as endearment toward my students, but which may have puzzled or challenged them when I spread my arms and asked, "You, the Future of Hungary, what will it be like here in fifty years?"

In this southern city bordering the former Yugoslavia, many adults remember shelling a few years ago. I met a man who barely survived the bombing of his apartment and was smuggled out of his country without wife, children, and aging parents because he would have been called up for service in the Yugoslav military the day his employment as manager of the television station ended, the day it was fire-bombed by the United Nations. One polyglot from Yugoslavia struck me in particular during interviews of incoming freshmen. The teachers want candidates who will not only learn English but make positive contributions to the class. As she listed languages she spoke—English, Slavic or Yugoslav, Russian, Hungarian (the teacher said no, she will have to learn Hungarian as well as improve her English)—she couldn't remember the name of that other language "just like English." Everyone looked puzzled. "Oh, German! I speak that too."

Kovacs Peter would still know some Russian and perhaps German for the tourists, but all in all he did not seem academic. I never saw him read while we camped out on adjacent hospital cots. Every other person in Hungary has a doctorate, but Peter was in the trades. He dressed impeccably, spent most of his life in our city, and was a manager when he retired. When the Russians went home, they left a debt and the deed to factories. No one stepped up with assistance, so the new government sold the factories to multinationals like *Nestle, Coca-Cola,* and *Tesco.* Kovacs Peter was disappointed at this drift of power, but he transferred into the new industries with a worker's ageless despair: as in the past, the worst is inevitable. Most retired are on state-assistance unwillingly and without tidy nest eggs.

Instead, many on the state dole have lost limbs, or are confined to wheelchairs due to workplace illnesses or injuries. A deeply felt national pride led them to hinder if not sabotage the plunder of Hungary's resources. Even after the fall of the Soviet Union, can openers, hand tools, or small appliances might as well have been sabotaged—how quickly and consistently they come apart in the consumer's hands. Before the Conservative Party was elected by a small majority in 1989, Victor Urban at a student protest in Budapest led thousands in chanting: "Russians Go Home!" The woman who told me so had been guiding her Russian tourists that day; they were vital to the Hungarian economy. She translated for her group; she said they all agreed.

Maybe Kovacs Peter was at that rally, but he would have been in his sixties. He may have ventured to Budapest to protest fifty years of Communism, cold war, and the iron curtain. He could recall the twilight of the Hapsburgs and the Holy Roman Empire from grandparents' stories, which bitterly condemned the Treaty of Trianon, settled on Hungary in 1920. Even today it causes resentment on the streets; every anniversary graffiti decry its injustice. This was the moment many contemporary Hungarians see as the greatest betrayal. Croatia and Austria were beneficiaries to the east, Yugoslavia to the south, while the newly established Romania cut across Hungary's eastern border and separated Hungarian families, no longer credited for Magyar heritage but ostracized, forbidden to speak their language or practice their customs. Hungary was predisposed in 1936 to accept Nazi offers of original boundary restoration when a Communist dictatorship led by Bela Kun came to power in 1919, the Hungarian middle class resenting its mostly Jewish leaders trained in Russia.

As a youngster Peter would have absorbed the culture of the Hapsburgs, and the warrior strain of the Magyars, fierce conquerors of the eastern plain. His family would have instilled the customs of the Dual Monarchy, whose seats were Vienna and Budapest. His educational opportunities, however, diminished when he turned nineteen as Hungary deepened its complicity with Nazi Germany. In 1939 it enacted anti-Semitic legislation to keep Jews from key occupations, and forbade sex between non-Jews and Jews, whose population numbered 825,000. After 1944 he witnessed mass deportations shrinking that number to 490,000. Until then, Regent Horthy had refused Hitler's demands; Hungary was unwilling to liquidate its people or embrace the Final Solution. Peter's generation experienced the influence of Hapsburg royalists, the fascist rule of the Nazis, the totalitarianism of the Communists, and the present democratically elected government.

In journal entries I felt my way through a detritus of cultural stimuli, unraveling an onion at the core of which was a cloud. How I misconceive the world is how I conceive of myself. This is what I was doing in my notebook for my first three weeks in Hungary, my health quietly deteriorating up to September eleventh.

August 24, 2001

There is a bell ringing at the Dom, the votive cathedral, built to fulfill the promise to the Almighty for saving the city from the great flood of 1879, which wiped out most buildings, some of which were standing since 1267 when the city was incorporated by Bela IV. But in 2000, cyanide tailings from an Australian goldmine in Romania floated downriver and all the bottom fish filled the city with their stench, choked the banks of the Tisza, and clogged the slow straightened current on its stately course to Yugoslavia. My students believe the river will always be polluted. We saw a pig float downstream.

In Szeged, the last Hungarian site along the Tisza, the river passes on its way to Beograd (Belgrade) to join the Duna (Danube) and flow to the Black Sea as border between Romania and the Ukraine; the city streets are rings of a tree growing out from its center. There may be a way to estimate age by counting streets and tram or bus lines to ascertain how recently they were developed into livable parts of the city to accommodate the development that took place during the Communist regime. Szeged's population grew during the Milosovic regime in Yugoslavia, and is now close to 200,000. My students live in tall building, flats I've heard Americans call basements in the sky.

Hungary was part of the Ottoman Empire for a hundred fifty years and Prince Suleiman among other Ottoman rulers, wanted to extend his holdings into Austria. Hungary was the line in the sand for Western Civilization, which allowed Turks to advance no closer to the center of Christendom in Rome. This wasn't the last time Hungary was hung out to dry, but the Turkish occupation from 1542 to 1686 begins a list showing Hungary was Western Europe's first line of defense. The Turkish occupiers began to straighten the Tisza for defense purposes, but after the great compromise, which produced the Austro-Hungarian Empire, Count Szecenyi made it his business to continue the project so that irrigation could foster arable land. Within ten years of completing his project, River Tisza flooded, and two days later the city was destroyed.

August 26, 2001

We wander streets which place us in the last century, or late in the previous, and notice how close the buildings, how dark the vines enclose what we would call, were we late 19th century French novelists, the narrow lanes as they abut the city walls. And whenever we enter a store down stone steps and approach the counter, beside which a small chain separates us from vegetables and fruit, greeted by the cashier—"jo napot kivanok," and point at plums (*sylvae*), peaches (*oszibarack*), eggs and orange juice (I don't know eggs, & *narancia*), each price written in a bold hand, my son likes to say we're in for a spot of grocery-store pointing.

The buildings are massive structures of stone, architectural designs common in Western Europe. Streets are named after poets most often, though some for politicians or

174

philanthropists as in America. The French helped with the design of the Dom, pride of Csongrad County, a daring architectural masterpiece, which on our first approach reminded me of Notre Dame. Victor Hugo Utca (street) lies in its shadow. Our building is in the grand style of the 19th Century: a balcony in the rear hangs over clianthus trees and joins balconies of neighbor buildings surrounding them, a garden without cultivation, while plants and bonsai trees adorn the balconies. The flat itself, large and with high ceilings, exemplifies utilitarian design within the framework of the fallen Hapsburgs.

In many places the regime arranged to have one or two families crowd together. Yet families with two or more children in flats like ours got automatic qualification for their own flat, no rent. Nine-foot-high double doors connect and close off each room and shut to allow gas heaters more efficiency. But the manner of finishing plaster, or mudded walls, exposed pipes, the sturdy little stove, sinks, tub, water heater, fridge, tiny washing machine (which I've dubbed "Stalin's mother" for its bouncing on the cement floor, and we apologized to the woman below): these all indicate choices—as do the rugs, dressers, cabinets—based on practicality more than aesthetics. It's interesting to see how the purely practical is compatible and unable to overwhelm the entirely aesthetic choices made after 1879, to curve, for instance, the joint where walls rush up twelve feet to the wide expanse of ceiling in each large room and long hallway. In the stark stairway, wide enough for the once ornate woodwork of a spiral staircase, is now mostly very practical cement, dust from the neighboring construction site making us cough on the way upstairs. A huge heavy wood door requiring an antique key three inches long reminds us all day, on its chain as it rubs against the leg: you are in another place, from another time.

August 25? 26?

The days are going by, but it can't be the 28th because school starts then. We need a calendar desperately, and American

175

newspapers. Without enough language to take care of simple things, we have no phone, cable, no toaster yet, teapot, no internet. Is there a state you reach at the beginning of culture shock, even before Week One is finished, where you don't want to learn the difficult language, become tired of everything taking forever? Where you detest helplessness, especially helplessness, more than anything else? Where you want to get a few things done; somehow for me, one who prefers the minimal, in this culture where salaries never rise to meet a person's even fabricated needs, I cannot just live Hungarian. I can't happily do with less. Nice motto. All right I'll forget about the toaster.

August 27

Hungarian is a one-of-a-kind language. Not spoken in other countries, it's survived a couple of thousand years. Everything is written in it—menus, postal notices, signs on my door downstairs that could mean anything—I hope not telling me be home tomorrow for a police inspection; we've had impromptu drop-bys of plainclothes officers who didn't speak English, insisting they look inside to find out, presumably, if we were harboring unregistered aliens from Yugoslavia, Romania, and points southeast. These exchanges are so unlike being a glorified tourist, which is more or less what I'd anticipated. The closest aspect of communication has become easiest to neglect—talking with my family in our mother tongue, those precious and rare moments when we're not too exhausted to talk, just talk, for the first time so foreign.

I wanted to write what my students said about their country, so I asked them to prepare speeches about what an American should know to be happy. I forget what they said. Mostly they wanted me to see the sights. The river Tisza and its parks, the theater, everything I discovered by walking around town, or from guide books my wife wisely purchased before we left America. But when I asked the next question, all of them were more enthusiastic and gave extensive answers and asked questions. I asked did they like America, and would they want to go if they could? Yes, they liked it. "Of course," they said, an expression used so often by English-speaking Hungarians I took it to mean, "Of course, you stupid asshole." Did they want to go? All. Except one. And she was adamant about staying in her country. Why did they want to go? America is the land of dreams, no? Anything can happen. You can succeed, be what you want, have money, freedom, meet interesting, exciting people. Have you met many movies stars? Do you know many famous people? Then they would ask did I know some Somebody I had never heard of— rap star, movie icon, model, *futbol* up-and-comer. And since I am from Seattle, how often do I talk to Bill Gates? I had tapped a nerve of American idolatry.

"Now wait just one cotton-pickin' minute!" I said, holding up my hand. Puzzlement, befuddled expression on the face of the nerdy boy in the front row, big round eyes on the girl with the low-cut blouse. "Teacher, teacher, what means this *codonepigging?*" The teachable moment! Unbridled intellectual curiosity. These young people see, or their parents see, that good jobs, or trips to Hollywood and the Gold Coast of Florida at spring break, depend on the acquisition of this language which is continuously throwing them curve balls, such as "curve balls," an expression necessitating an elucidation of the art of baseball including gloves, bats, trophies, books, hats, balls, and a makeshift game on the overgrown tennis court.

Then we got back to misconceptions, or so I thought. My patriotism is often tarnished by the imperial disregard of Americans abroad, or arrogance, as if Divine Right, of politicos who proclaim even on foreign soil that ours is the "greatest nation on earth." I have felt it my duty to disabuse students of idealism. It isn't fair. Opining their belief in utopian America is my misconception. I insisted on telling anyone who listened, Hungarians are freer than Americans strapped to their houses,

177

dogs, yachts, cars, and debt to the eyeballs. To construe America as the land where anything can happen is not farfetched. I remember watching planes land in 1956 with Hungarian refugees in black and white TV news clips. A girl from Hungary, suddenly new in my fifth-grade class, was just as tentative about language and customs as my eager students today and just as horrified to offend. After the November debacle near the Hungarian Parliament where Russian tanks growled through the now pleasant streets not a block from the Danube, and where thousands were killed—the spray of bullets memorialized by bronze dots on the walls—Khrushchev's violent totalitarianism shocked the world more than the horrors of Stalin he revealed, though Auschwitz would weigh on the West for the balance of the century. In those days more than 200,000 Hungarians came to the West by way of Austria, but for the few weeks of the October rebellion, Hungarians assumed the United States would intercede, that our military would cross their borders and protect them from the Russian army, which suppressed the revolution on November 4th with 150,000 troops.

So, in fact, did Hungarian Jews at Auschwitz and Jewish leaders globally who expected and encouraged Roosevelt to strafe the ovens, although Nazi officers depended on the Geneva Convention, which forbade the bombing of concentration camps. The United States and United Kingdom had already refused to help Romanian refugees whose army had shot 60,000 people. When asked in Switzerland about the rising number of Jewish deaths in Europe, John Foster Dulles said it "doesn't matter." In 1944 and 1945 the Jewish council leadership, aware of the Holocaust, didn't warn their communities; historians speculate they believed cooperation with Germany would protect people. Two thousand five hundred wealthy Jews, however, were evacuated from Hungary. In his recent movie, *Amen*, the controversial director, Costa-Gavras takes on the well-documented silence of Pope Pius XII. Like many patriotic Germans shown in the film, the Pope, his handlers, and the

American ambassador seemed to find the staggering numbers and lightning efficiency beyond belief. A film made in Budapest, *Goodbye, Mr. Wallenberg*, gives these statistics regarding the Nazi deportations and executions in that city alone: "Adolph Karl Eichmann arrived with a staff of thirteen. Seven weeks later, 422,602 people were dead."

Because deportations didn't begin until late in the war and were mostly confined to those weeks in 1944, when Kovacs Peter would have been in his mid-twenties, and when Regent Horthy had abdicated his veto power, many Hungarian Jews lived who might otherwise have been gassed at Auschwitz or other death camps. The Russian liberators who gained control of Hungary were no better; *The Black Book of Communism* compares persecutions and exterminations between 1946 and 1989 with the ravages of Nazism. Perhaps those days were for Kovacs Peter the end of hope, his countenance fixed in acceptance. The future will be no better than the past, but we have these days, we have our health today if not tomorrow, children, our grandchildren— I saw it on his face in the hospital, and in the window of a passing tram, and repeated on faces of passengers, and on our street the plodding older men and women, or in the vigorous strides of those whose futures meant no change or dreams. I did not see it in my students' faces.

I noticed everybody's misconceptions but my own. I thought cultural difference exaggerated. Hungarian ways were Eastern Bloc solutions to problems already solved by other techniques. Magyarul, a member of the Finno-Ugric linguistic family, sharing some twenty words with the Finns, seemed an amalgam of Western languages, a made-up form. Hungarian cultural difference evaporated until I was left with problems and solutions. The architecture, transportation, cooking, art, music, even the educational system in which I was immersed struck me as not dissimilar enough to their counterparts in the West to be construed as a culture. I lived with this misconception of culture as something distinct from political difference for quite

179

some time during my stay, until I came to see Hungary's political history as simply the way this story goes. Culture itself abides in the people, generation by generation for over a thousand years. Not only problem solving, the measure of any political system, but celebration, loss, yearning, aspiration, and acquiescence make up a culture.

August 29

To register for the Residence Permit, a foreign national must go to the police station, and there meet perhaps a young woman who may not want to be a bureaucrat but such is her fate, and who suffers from allergies like many Hungarians and must pause frequently to blow her nose, and who speaks extremely fast as if terribly impatient with your not having known to provide each of the variety of receipts and written assurances the State requires her to assess. One can fume about the bureaucrats—how you could bank on their behavior, an exaggeration of U.S. bureaucratic scripts, perhaps made more intense by the fast foreign sounds, but paperwork itself may cause nastiness. What this young woman says zooms past me untranslated; papers whirl like pigeons in a storm. Maybe it's frustration with stupid people, ignoramuses like those issuing the State's requirements, or me. Nevertheless, it comes down to one person making choices.

I am a bureaucrat; endless paper shuffling makes me one. An iron door I need not explain, the state and the school demand demonstrations of knowledge: pass this test, receive a grade. Nothing to be done, Samuel Beckett's Vladimir sighs, as do teachers. Yet the way things were done under Communists eleven years ago, as one Yugoslav boy said, is the way of embryonic capitalists in the new Hungary. The government can be replaced, but the system itself follows tried and true methods. Who represents the State has power, which demeans the subject, or so the subjective reaction might go, which of course means nothing to the State. The very term "Communist bureaucracy" implies layers of Kafkaesque evasions, which inevitably secure the power of the State, no matter what its philosophy. Kafka after all was a subject of the Empire, not the Proletariat.

Why shouldn't a country like Hungary make it difficult for foreigners, specifically Americans, to come here? We were not all that helpful when multinationals bought the industrial plants and centers of power and business as the first non-communist government in fifty years denationalized its holdings to afford the cost of governing. Certainly someone like me, whose travel expenses and living accommodations are the direct result of a parliamentary decree, may further devalue the Hungarian forint. Although I part with American bucks here, I could be taking employment and housing away from Hungarians, who could do the job better. Many teachers and students here have traveled to Amerika. Our movies and celebrities are everywhere, selling global products. The State mandates bilingual schools. They must hire people for whom English is their birthright. This grants a surprise dignity to millions of Americans for whom some however neglected expertise places them also in the category of "native speaker." For some of us, no other language and literature has opened its heart quite so lovingly, yet we scramble to remember grammar rules and names of tenses dredged up from Latin class thirty-five years ago.

So why should the bureaucrat in the Residence Permit office look kindly on my application? Why shouldn't she pull out all the stops and harangue me in shrill staccato? What am I but an importer of—and god forbid she'd still say it—capitalist falsehoods? What do I offer but "Angolul," the value of which has already been proven; not world peace or its cultivation, but urban sprawl, slurred morality, dumb and dumber children, young adults, presidents, and addiction to the lazy grammar of greed?

Sometime in September

If I wanted to feel less self-important, I couldn't have picked a better thing to do than make myself a foreigner. I don't

181

know how they know, but they do. Maybe it's my features, my white hair, my clothes, posture, whatever— but they seem to know before I open my mouth I'm just a kid from Dorchester who found his way into a relatively fat salary and wound up here. It's not only the limitations of language, though that all-pervasive factor humbles me. It's the unfamiliarity—typical tourist difficulties with money, maps, grocery-store pointing, restaurant ordering and the giant tips I've given when I didn't intend to; I won't return for a month to give them time to forget my face or hire a new waiter. But the things I'd thought would give me prestige or an edge seem not to work. I am a poet (the Hungarian word is *kulto*, but I can't pronounce it). Maybe later I'll know that famous Central European respect for poets. The two anthologies I've read collect dead Hungarian poets, but it's hard to know if the same awe extends to contemporaries. The former president was a novelist, and poets' names become street names and the names of schools, and the statues of the national poet Petofi and others abound and are graced with flowers as was the plaque to Gyorg Babits today. It's still hard to evince whether respect for fallen heroes renowned for poetry is respect for poets, especially when Hungary embraces democracy and free-range capitalism. Within these political changes it may be that those voices speaking out against the repressions of democracy are overlooked, discounted as cranks, youthful protesters, or non-existent, and that poets of love, environment, friendship never measure up—even poets of protest or war— to those of the past in the view of the popular taste, sophisticated enough to admire Miklos Radnoti whose beautiful poetry rivals Neruda's best work from the same period, the 1930s and '40s.

September 8
We are not yet as homesick as the poor Hungarian Fulbright family in Nebraska who have already tied a rope with knots for every week away and keep a Sunday evening untying ceremony.

I arrived late for my violin lesson—yes, violin:at fifty-five I've come to think it might be better to go down swinging—and sat outside on the bench while Gyorgy played inside the practice room. I might have thought a student was playing but for how complicated the piece was and how well played. After a few minutes he opened the door and invited me in. He was rehearsing for an upcoming performance here at the *zeneiskola*, the music school, in the recital on Women's Day. I like taking lessons from him. The language difference has become less a barrier than a tool. He brings his dictionary to our lessons and sometimes I bring mine. When he wants me to relax my posture or nervous grip on the instrument or bow, he says, "Be lazy, lazy . . . ." At first I tried to correct him, but I prefer his expression to any other.

I assume Kovacs Peter plays an instrument, at least in private; at least he did once, and attended a school like this *zeneiskola*. Once he had a visitor, a girl of high school age. She must have been a granddaughter. She was very nice, saying hello to me and a few polite English phrases. Clearly she was fluent in both languages, but didn't want to intrude with a conversation. I was two feet away from them, trying to keep aloof.

September 11, 2001

Today was Women's Day, when men give women flowers. The staff divided by silent command into males and females on either side of the room. Staff and students love the young principal, who speaks no English and has such an elegant voice my son commented on it. He read a poem by the national poet, Jozsef Attila, the room instantly hushed. The rhythms of this language enchant us, the poem short, lilting. After reading it, he asked the male teachers to take the many potted geraniums arranged in circles on the tables and give them to the women teachers; then would everyone please have a glass of champagne. As they passed out the flowers, they kissed each woman on both

183

cheeks. This was at noon, the students in the halls between classes. The teachers who still had classes went back and taught. I was done for the day, and went off to buy my wife a flower.

What if Peter was in the Arrow Cross? It is perhaps impossible to imagine the past of someone we respect to have been heinous or bereft of humanity. We think it highly unlikely, or out of character. We think he could never have done such a thing. We think his meek demeanor, his obvious kindness, even his facial expression, which we interpret as both acceptance of whatever suffering history may have in store for him, and regret for those he has survived, as indications of a character too compassionate to have rounded up and deported Jews in such vast numbers and with such speed as the Nazis and their Hungarian collaborators, the Arrow Cross Party. To imagine Kovacs Peter in that bleak uniform fitting him perfectly, his younger face framed in the regulation hat and tight gray collar and black tie, to imagine him in high boots and maybe gloves, one of which he might have had to remove writing down the particulars of an investigation: I cannot see him this way. My impression was of a man whose kindness was simply kindness, not the result of a character formed by committing horrific acts of bureaucracy such as taking names, listing items of entire households for storage, or as happened, shipment to other households where the stain of racial impurity could not diminish their worth. I cannot imagine it was his fate to enlist in Arrow Cross, though he may have been press-ganged to act as underling. Just as I can't imagine he collaborated with the Communist Secret Police. The House of Terror, now a museum, the *Terrorhaza* on Andrassy Boulevard in Budapest, a few hundred yards from Octagon Square, is where people passed but heard no screams, or did and kept walking. He could not be the same man, so gentle, and have assisted torture. In the same building both Nazis and Communists destroyed or ended the lives of thousands. But isn't

184

it possible that a gentle person can be cruel? Isn't it possible a gentle population has cruelty in its past? Can't quiet citizens follow rules of etiquette and breeding and believe 400,000 must be exterminated?

As we waited in line outside the House of Terror, our tour guide couldn't suppress her distaste for the newly elected socialist government. The House itself, I understand, was designed by a Hollywood set designer, so gimmicky I don't think I was the only American who felt manipulated by music and atmosphere. How different from Auschwitz, which was more straightforward, offering evidence in the stark halls, cold cells, and gas chambers. No haunting music, no artistic renditions. Many in the new government are former Communists and some, I heard it rumored, may have committed atrocities the museum depicts. An American said they should simply acknowledge complicity in torture before taking elected office. Despite the manipulative atmosphere, I'm convinced many were guilty of crimes against humanity, and should be prosecuted and sentenced if found guilty.

Though the Arrow Cross was largely volunteer, they were excessively brutal. Peter, had he been among their ranks, might have supervised labor battalions. Many Jews were saved from deportation, only to be brutalized by the Hungarian military. Many were killed or maimed while clearing mine fields. No mass killings of Hungarians are recorded. I prefer to think that Peter, in whatever capacity he served during the war, was among those who helped Jews to hide or escape. Members of the Catholic Church, for instance, some members of the Arrow Cross, and famously Raoul Wallenberg risked and sacrificed their lives out of respect for the humanity terrorized in their presence. Later, there were Communist collaborators who reported on their neighbors or taped phone conversations of people in the next flat because a son's or daughter's university degree was put in jeopardy. A quiet people, a gentle people, even a polite people—of which Kovacs Peter seems the epitome—may face a grim deed in order for the next day, week, or month to arrive without disturbance, and do what they must with seemliness and decorum.

No, I can't believe Peter was in the Arrow Cross. Thousands protested on Castle Hill in Budapest the reelection of the Communists, as thousands waited days to get into the House of Terror. From his eyes, there could be no forgiving, nor remorse, nor vengeance or hatred. His face told me what most of his countrymen seemed to feel: the long road we are on has few surprises but beauty.

Klinika, Szegedi Union, September 13, 2001
I'm not sure of the name of this place. I don't know where I am, or how, after all the best intentions and trying to be practical about the atrial fibrillation I am prone to, I have wound up in—though it seems a prison—a ward on the second floor of the hospital which services our district. I feel like a prisoner perhaps because for days now I've been frustrated in my attempts to get the Residence Permit, which seemed so all-important, which would give us a relative degree of freedom: phone, internet, cable, and library card. We've been here twenty-four days, and these last few I think I know a little about what it's like to live within a Communist regime. Deep in layers of behavior things move slowly or don't change, or can't, won't, will always be thus, so get used to it, no matter the consequences.

My doctor tells me the arhythmia began on September 11, an appropriate response to the devastation at home. I was affected by what I saw on Hungarian TV, but without numbers, proportions, or commentary in English, I couldn't piece together the sequence or assign responsibility. Now I am imprisoned by chemicals that short-circuited my heart, and by my doctor's schedule. American hospitals get patients out quickly, here rest is advised. My own thinking is that getting the hell out of here can't be too soon. I am seething at fate. I should walk out— fourteen beds and all old men who shuffle past without a glance.

I'm sure it would be rude to do so, but I'm craving contact with someone in a similar fix. In a ten-by-eight cell which I share with a man who hasn't acknowledged me and who appears very sickly, about seventy, and snores, I'm cut off from my wife and son, from news of America where the entire earth has focused attention, where yesterday a three-minute silence was observed for the jihad victims in New York and D.C. and all over Europe as well. Cut off too from my family and friends in the U.S. Cultural difference, medical difference, politics, political history has led me to break habits of despair, and rebel against my unnecessary spirit of acceptance. Outside, horns blare because more young Hungarians got married; it must be Saturday.

I wonder if Kovacs Peter is among those who today deny the Holocaust took place. As in many countries there are those who view this horrifying epoch with extreme concern, and those indifferent or who deem statistics irrelevant to their country's future, and those who claim it is a lie. Hungary's right wing republished Nazi literature and Hitler's diatribes. On the other hand, the Holocaust has been taught in the schools since 1989, and there is a scholarly debate about its significance for Hungarians. It is only the fringe groups who deny it ever happened, and, though I couldn't speak a word to Peter, I cannot believe he would have denied it. I do, however, see that he would consider it less relevant than the Communist legacy which finally came to dominate every aspect of life, including marriage, parenthood, and honor, the essence in fact of totalitarian rule.

Is it racist to ignore or deny its significance? Hungarians seemed unwilling to indulge the depth of sadness which must accompany such a discussion. In America, we cannot imagine such suffering. September 11th pales in proportion, and has already, for most of us, disappeared into the realm of doctrinaire politics and mythological patriotism. We understand the abstract, the affront of being challenged and hurt on our own soil, but only those who have lost family seem capable of grasping the deep sadness such an event entails for the nature of humankind.

Racism in Hungary seemed to me widely acknowledged in the majority relationship to the Gypsies, a national issue which the society is seeking to heal. Hungary's Gypsy population, like that of many European nations, was horribly victimized in the Holocaust, as it has been throughout history. Many may have survived because they entertained both Germans and Hungarians, Gypsy music still a major cultural heritage. Yet racism toward Gypsies was strong among the Nazis and their supporters like Arrow Cross. The putative number of Gypsy victims, five thousand, was much lower than Jewish victims because they rarely registered.

I found it a touchy subject with some of my students, and one that, when I asked about it, started a vehement debate. There were Gypsy students in our school who passed for "white" and went unnoticed, but Gypsies have their own schools, their own society. I found them on the streets or in the malls and subways of Budapest. Some could speak English and had tales of drunkenness and unemployment, crime and ill health.

September 15 Omanyi Egyetem Klinikai Szeged
Still arrhythmic. Lightning has passed over the town. A light and steady rain. Now will I sleep? The two most active patients are standing in their robes, talking on the other side of the ward. The most restless is beside the nurse's station, a sink and table, the bold light bulb, towels, plastic things with blood on them piled up. The male nurse, who wears a protective facemask to ward off germs apparently, drips blood on my sheet when he removes the intravenous needle for the saline solution. There's no toilet paper.

September 16 Klinikai Szeged 8.05 a.m.
Still fibrillated.

On the morning of September 12 hardly anyone talked to me as I came into school, went to my desk, got the classroom key and met my students in the hall. A few other teachers and some of the students could tell me the latest estimates of the number dead, but no one knew much for certain. It was even unclear about the planes crashing into the towers. As their only American, I had to address my students in the first period. I don't know if the doctor was right in saying my heart began skipping beats then, in that hour. The atrial fibrillation certainly is debilitating, and can be triggered by stress, cause difficulty breathing or walking around. Not a good physical problem for a presidential candidate; Bill Bradley quit the race against Gore because of it. Some said Gore must have felt relief on September 12, that the chads and the courts hadn't swung his way. Though atrial fibrillation can make life difficult for a leader, in hindsight we might do better with someone whose mortality is more in the forefront. Bush, of course, is healthy as a horse, but Cheney, perhaps the only one in that administration with a serious heart problem, at least has a heart, albeit mechanical.

When I talked to my class, I told how upset and confused I was, but I also said that Americans will seek revenge and that it will be terrible. Perhaps Osama bin Laden had been blamed by then, but I don't think so. This was several months prior to our noticing jets manoeuvre over Hungary in the direction of Afghanistan.

9.45 a.m.

The ward goes into its first round of activity at 5:00 a.m. Lights went on and the two nurses, one male, one female, emerged from the last cell, the curtain drawn, and began administering pills, injections, and IVs. I don't think the nurse got to me until around six. She injected me with of some sort of blood thinner in the abdomen. Weird feeling.

189

There are ten men here including me. I'm younger and spryer than the rest. The room is wide open, dormitory style, broken into seven cells of two beds each. The glass brick walls allow light from the nurse's station to glow into each cell all night.

I've only noticed one cell closed with a green curtain for a few minutes. No privacy. The ward, as my doctor predicted, takes me back in time several decades. "Centuries," he joked, criticizing the slow progress. He spent a year at Johns Hopkins in the early '90s and he thinks the Klinikai is not up to the American level even at that time. My father in the hospital back home was in a room by himself with a TV, a phone in his name, his mail delivered, and a private bathroom. Several nurses checked on him, bathed him, changed his bedding, and spoke in cooing tones in his own language, though he ranted and insulted them.

Maybe the biggest activity of the other nine is urination. Three men I can see from my bed need to use the bottle deposited in a rack below the bed. The bed is a solid metal frame less than one meter by three meters. My head and feet touch the boards. There are no springs, just a thin foam mattress on hard wire frame. Fortunately, the man next to me who has a sweet smile and generously offered a banana last night, doesn't use the urine bottle. He gets up and walks around and seems to use the toilet. The toilet alone would violate U.S. health laws. It is repulsive beyond polite efforts to describe. The smell from labelled, half-filled urine sample bottles and toilets which don't flush dominates the floor.

Smells: on top of the urine, or mixing with it, is the continuous wafting of cigarette smoke from somewhere. Patients smoke in the toilet: nurses, doctors, visitors, other patients past the entry to this ward. There is always cigarette smoke; wheeled through the emergency room, I smelled it. When wheeled into the radiologist, a striking blond woman whose English at first sounded good, her directions to hold my breath for the x-ray were the more literal translation or more primitive meaning of breath, as "pneuma" in Greek: "No smoking!" "No breathing?" I asked, and she corrected herself, but I like her version better. Medicinal smells, the smell of bread—three slices and a slab of breakfast spam— the clean soap Kathy used in the Stalin's mother washing machine on the white T-shirt and shorts I'm wearing today because I don't have old man pajamas like the others— dark blue, pale blue, stripes with T-shirts at the collars. Good leather slippers.

There is camaraderie among them I'm unable to enter. I won't be able to. Even beyond the language barrier, their compassion for one another has more to do with age and infirmity. They may know that I will be here a short time; my ailment is urgent, but I'm not the high risk of, did he say "thrombus"? which I translate as "stroke." Otherwise I am refusing to be sick and I have use of my motor functions. Compassion for someone with my symptoms—and a rich American – may be wasted or unnecessary. Instead what I see, especially with my cell mate, Kovacs Peter, is the grace and ease with which he strolls about and chats with the two more talkative guys maybe ten years his junior. He's friendly, though a little diffident, and more confident than they, managerial. Last night before bedtime the very old man across the ward from our cell, who seems the weakest, shuffled off to the toilet, which took a long time in itself—getting up, putting on slippers, standing—shuffling seemed a bit faster than standing still, just—and didn't return.

Thirty minutes later I understood little of what Kovacs Peter and the two younger men were saying, enough to know they were concerned about the older man. A few moments later Kovacs Peter was leading him back from the WC. They moved stately, both shuffling. He let him rest his hand in the crook of his own arm, and when they arrived at the man's bed, Peter carefully unfurled the blanket, smoothed his sheet, helped him off with his slippers, helped him lift his legs into the bed, covered him over with the blanket so very gently, tucking the old infirm

191

man into his bed as if he himself were a pillar of strength, and then went off to use the toilet which I assume he'd been waiting to do for an hour.

September 16, 9.03 p.m.

Still irregular pulse, I think, although now I feel somewhat weaker, maybe from all the blood thinning. I wonder, finally, if I have come here to relax. Only my recent bad attitude makes me qualify for what we have continuously referred to as cultural difference here in Hungary. What is the generosity, after all? Kovacs Peter is a good example. Many people have offered their help, while many have kept their distance. Certainly no cultural trait. It could be the product of politics. Peter and the men here in this ward are products of an array of cultural influences. A much older man who yesterday seemed hardly able to stand in the WC (pronounced Veetzee) and today walked off the ward, all dressed, dapper in his hat, wife grimly following, stopped before my bed and wished me good health. They all experienced the Communist regime, could describe October, 1956, the Change and the last decade and a half. Twentieth century political history, a product of cultural history, of choices leaders made, brought about success and failure which allow them to be either generous or standoffish, or perhaps shy and timid with Americans. I should at least try to converse. Why have I come here?

September 17 8.40 a.m., Klinikai Szegedi, Monday morning.

A test which sounds like echocardiogram, but they have to put something down my esophagus like the video camera the American doctors rammed up my ass to see if I had colon cancer. With this one, they want to be sure I don't vomit on them while they search for signs of clotting. I wasn't eating anything after I saw the young orderly, a handsome and active teenager, carry four filled urine bottles away without gloves. He served my first slab of dinner spam, so I decided not to eat if he served anything

192

else. But it was a different guy this morning. That young fellow came on last night about six or seven. And his girlfriend sat on her bike outside, and waved to him for quite a while. I hope he washed his hands before touching her.

9.30 a.m.

Doctors walk around the ward with students and stop by each bed: this one has pulmonary dysfunction, this one bladder, this one gastrointestinal, and this one has a writing problem which we will drain by bleeding twice a day, the stupid Amerikai.

10 a.m.

The doctor who just examined me seemed so careful. They all do. But this doctor's English seemed judicious. He was tall and elegant, precise and articulate, although he spoke with exaggerated economy. And he seemed wealthy somehow—a gold pen and the clean aftershave smell on his hands. "You know you are programmed for today" was the last thing he said to me. And gave his half smile, somewhat mysterious, before he and the others took off on further rounds. "Programmed?" No, I didn't know that, and had no time to tell him that I didn't understand, and no one else to tell.

1.45 p.m.

On their rounds about ten students got to listen to the beat of my heart. Odd, their tentative laying on of stethoscopes to my bared chest. The curtain half closed, they can enter one at a time; like a sideshow circus freak, I lay here with my little heartbeat, my shirt pulled up. They're discussing now what they've heard and asking if there was a murmur. Sell tickets next time. Come one come all! The spastic heart boy! See him lie down, hear his silly thump.

193

The last time I saw him he was virtually invisible—he wasn't in the scene. It was in the Dom Ter, that open square, almost an acre of rounded stones and surrounded by the cathedral, tall and imposing with its two towers and university buildings, statuary, sculpted figures lining the portico, busts of professors, musicians, poets, artists, and clergymen who over the centuries had earned the nation's gratitude. Everything gray and people walking along the edges of the courtyard. It was a rainy day in the middle of February about as bleak as it gets, but it must have been much worse in the middle of Communist winters when someone would come to this slab for solace. Kovacs Peter was walking along the stone perimeter, white hair slick as a skullcap, beige windbreaker, sensible shoes, his gaze turned down, furtive yet dignified. At the arch he entered Dom Ter to hear the bells and watch the fifteen-minute dance of Saint Stephen and all his attendant saints and soldiers in the beautiful clock above the square, where their painted life-size sculptures emerge at 11:45 every morning in slow procession motoring on a track into the daylight through three creaking doors, the bells out of tune. His serious face, a long and penetrating glare of compassion toward our little tragedy: these things happen, we move on, life has no resolution. He was the man who told the porter at the university building to call the ambulance for my son, who helped my son stand up, and carried the bicycle inside where the porter kept it for me. Couldn't speak English, but luckily a doctor showed up and assisted with translation. The porter wanted me to describe the bike before he'd let me take it. He told me that a man had come in to say a little boy was outside bleeding from his head. The man stayed long enough for the ambulance to arrive and take my son to the children's wing of the Klinikai, and then sauntered off through that arched entrance to Dom Ter. "Was he a tall man, white hair combed back, sharp features, a bit frail, angular nose casting a look of profound resignation?" Yes,

194

translated the doctor, but I already recognized the affirmative, Yes, *Igen, Igen.*

2.45 p.m.
    It's very disturbing to me that I can't remember passing out in the office. A young woman, the anesthesiologist, sprayed something horrible too far down my throat and jabbed me in my arm. Later, something big was removed from my mouth, but I don't recall getting back in the wheelchair, or being wheeled back except it was a shorter trip. They must have knocked me out.

3.50 p.m.
    Dr Rostozi Janos tells me the drug has an amnesiac effect. Did the KGB invent it? CIA?
    Teddy brought music he knows I like. The one that makes everything utterly right is "Birth of the Cool." So I start to listen, and watch men saunter past, nurses and afternoon visitors. I must look odd, stretched on my hard bed with headphones and notebook on my lap, nodding to bebop, writing in trance. I really don't care; the churlishness of a prisoner has set in and I have begun to behave in ways conflicting with my dignified station in life, and slightly irrational. As I listen to "Deception," the whole room floats. Buttons on a dress, deep blue and nonchalant:

With every kiss I throw
I know the wide boat on a sea of funny faces.
Laugh at me, boys,
I'm climbing up the string of broken sticks
to wed the scent of love.
Up up and up the New York windows
sail the walls of sound.

Nothing so pure.
Dogs bark.

195

They move their chains to stand around the table.

This feels true,
each time I know your face
rhythm of my heart, a music I don't care how divine,
fills the hills with roses, where can I go?
But I fall down, a tumble of cloth ending in one
plink of the keys.
So this is fullness.

9.03 p.m.

      Slipped into regular sinus rhythm at about six tonight. I have to stay most of the day either because of the doctor's schedule or I needed to rest, is what they'll tell me. I hope I can say something to Kovacs Peter, at least goodbye—*Viszontlataszra*—and shake his hand before I walk out.

I came back months later—the medicine didn't take. I was within 24 hours of the arrhythmia, so they kept me overnight, but I woke still arrhythmic, and they took what I consider drastic measures—which they couldn't do after 24 hours. They wheeled me into the Cardiovascular, where patients were dying inside clear plastic wrappers. They shaved my chest, knocked me out, and administered paddles as on every TV emergency show before losing the patient, someone's brother, boyfriend, son, mother, me. I woke again with no memory moments later, my heart back to normal and two red marks on my ribcage like stains our small iron leaves when I use it on my shirts.

WILD ART

In school the hallway noises are always indistinguishable.
Yet behind the students joking or the occasional clear utterance
emerging from the crowd, friction of clothing and flap of rubber
soles on the marble floors, there is faithful silence. This old
building was designed to enclose it. Its most common
interruption is a door shutting, either nearby or far down the
hall, a two-beat iambic ending with a thud—*ta-tum*—sudden
and defined. Since beginning these few sentences, at least twenty
such *ta-tums* have gone off somewhere on the floor, the last far
away like retreating gunfire. The door to my room is ajar because
the student suspense when it creaks open is a greater distraction,
and because the air in this room gets so bad they complain. Two
beats, and silence which can't be taught or trained. The sigh of
the heater this morning because the room was so cold, a purr
that covers for a real silence in which even the friction of walking
becomes disturbing, the click of a three-ring binder, the door,
students as if in a passing parade: these go pretty much unnoticed
unless someone making noise tries to get attention. For my
poetry students who brought headphones to try to write while
tapping out somebody else's beat, these yips of things do not
become the matter through which sound in the poem weaves.
Nor this tiny plastic clicking along the stone hall until a small
orange triangle stops before the door. Three kids playing some
odd kick-the-candy game pass by the classrooms. And then,
beauty of freshman bluntness, five boys all turn, dark in heavy
coats, baseball-behatted, squatting on the bench someone moved
into the hall and above which someone hung a stolen bus stop
sign, and point as one body in silence to give up the boy standing

197

and guilty in a white and orange ski jacket, and then groan that the entire group must go outside.

When the silence of the hall is back, there's only a stifled sneeze; somebody in a blue hat trudges by, his boot a softer thud than three doors closing across the hall. The attendance girl's soft soles whisper three times past my door. School may be the most silent place students know. Two kids today, a freshman boy and girl, tied themselves together at the ear by a black headphone cord. Do they ever know real silence, or listen for it? An inner voice we're made to pay attention to becomes incessantly boring. Another class saunters along the hall as if to an insignificant event, library research; they unintentionally call the minds of twenty or thirty, perhaps a hundred other students out of reverie and personal delight. The word "silence" in high school notebooks is synonymous with "boredom," but this is only the shorthand. For instance, among Freshman English students discussing the value of silence, someone shouts "boring" right away without fail in each class discussion of the topic. Nothing's happening. The ten kids in poetry class don't feel that way, although they utter identical responses. Five of them are in class, the others absent or skipping. Someone runs up the stone stairs at the north end of the hall and lopes by the open door at a quiet trot. Another catches his breath and slows down, shoes quiet as sticky sponges; how aware he seems of entering pools of sound without causing a ripple. To interrupt the poetry class and ask them to write about "silence" would be to cause them to resent the intrusion before they would begin perhaps on a different subject. The discussion would be pointless for different reasons with the thirty freshmen whose usually shorter attention spans reinforce the argument that silence implies nothing going on, or that no attention-fixing educational gimmickry is taking place, so why can't we enjoy one another's fabulous wit?

Can silence be valuable to anyone but the teacher for whom it is relief from being the constant target of public opinion or else a chance to grade papers? Yet whenever teachers see this time without the noises of teaching the class as an opportunity to experience silence for its own sake, to restore the privacy of thought, an act which students could emulate, they feel they're stealing time and may sometimes feel guilty. The busy-ness of being a teacher seems always to involve going some place "off the floor," in the language of Department Store Knowledge, to get yet another piece of paper which will in all likelihood contain incomplete information. Do teachers themselves ever know real silence, perhaps the one word which people most often associate with teachers and librarians? Certainly we know relative meanings. "The lack of disturbance" may be a kind of teacherly definition to imply its usefulness in educational settings.

"Disturbance," however, is already a lack, or at least diminished powers of concentration. Where a concentration of certain forces may result in, say, a placid lake, another form of concentration—wind, storm, rain, hail—could diminish placidity but not overwhelm it; noises while the class writes or reads do not really break silence, or disturb, until they surpass the students' concentration on work. But the teacher, ever vigilant, concerned, charged to protect levels of concentration rare at a certain age, the teacher has difficulty ignoring noises which don't affect the entire class, harbingers of chaos and distraction. White noise in class may be storm warnings. During a class period where student concentration may be at its height, in writing or reading, the one or two who have difficulty with any work draw the teacher away from the experience of silence. The teacher's function, we might believe, is to move around the room and help, not indulge in personal reverie. Certainly the teacher must be available as a resource. When classes read as a group once a week, everyone will actually read only if the teacher sits up front, eyes glued to a book, enjoying reading and indulging this joy in front of the class. For me, on days I don't do this, frankly all hell breaks loose. My classroom seems to be coming apart, my nerves wearing thin, my inner teacherly voice constantly suggesting I get things under control both to protect

199

students who in fact are concentrating and to demand everyone learn. Is the preconception of placidity as disturbing as sudden changes in weather which cause the lake to appear in confusion? Isn't confusion only not seeing an event? The concepts of any class discussion are like random influences of weather such that the climatology—eons described as stormy, placid, disruptive, calm, heavenly, chaotic, or life-threatening—is as important as course content, the material, the landscape of a course over which we seem to have some control by its nature as a construct. Classroom management, on the other hand, employing as necessary judicious amounts of relative silence, attempts to direct the unpredictable, even the uncontrollable at the edge of things, a chaos about to disrupt the environment. We manage based on the bias that some humans can control others. We could say that more of the desired kind of learning happens in the "heavenly" classroom climate than the "chaotic." In either, the Very Silent never talk or volunteer, never complain, and exemplify indifference; whatever is non-essential, the only necessity is to wait. The bell will ring; the quarter, semester, year, high school itself will be over and whatever is of real interest or significance, and in certain cases there may be no such thing, will arise. These students believe they need only show up. They are attendees more than they are students. Their silence is rooted in depression. Stillness for them is not akin to Buddhist emptiness, but to being stuck to a kind of immobility shaping a world around the soul into permanent ceaseless drone. This is not silence, but the thick clogging of the ears that drowning or asphyxiated people know.

Silence in the student's life can become a practice, a way of addressing the world. The most capable students have that quality which allows them to move unimpeded by biases and burdens of previous bad or difficult educational experiences. They are the ones for whom the great parade passes in the hall as well as at the front of the room where a teacher talks or writes on the board. All of their moments attending to their own educations give them those opportunities to acquire what

200

they need. Not distracted by the hall or the white noise, the incomplete information the teacher or textbooks occasionally provide, they have silenced that voice with which others tune out real ideas. They give themselves over to each moment and take what is there. They may often be observers, or the more careful participants, in any class arrangement. By silencing biases which conflict with their own acts of learning, they consciously take control of education and themselves. They embody the word "student," from the Latin *studere*, to be eager, earnest, to take pains, to strive after. The word implies zeal. Shocking to think of our classrooms training zealots given the pejorative connotations of a word now associated with terrorism. Yet like a fanatic, a student is one whose enthusiasm for learning is so great nothing can derail it. No one who demands that this student learn according to prescription will be completely satisfied with the result, a knowledge rich and inspired, gained while silencing plaintive voices taught in fact by public school. Education makes demands on students. Those demands are specific to each course where only the teacher determines whether the student meets them. Student knowledge which depends on teacher instruction creates personal characteristics in all students. In some, the need to rebel, in others the depressed silence mentioned earlier. In many, the need to know exactly what the teacher wants in order to attain enough points for the desired grade. When something is lacking—information hard to find in the library, for instance, pencil sharpener non-functioning, conflicting definitions in the dictionary—many will instantly fall back on the learned voice of complaint. The tones escalate as the problem increases— receiving an A-minus instead of A can lead to major confrontations between a teacher and a student trained to make school responsible for education and a grade the result of prescribed behaviors. This institutional thinking is the most common lack of independence among students. It is acceptable because teachers assume responsibility for grades. Despite the worn response, "You gave yourself this grade," or, "This is the grade your work deserves," it is the teacher who evaluates based on a number of human interactions, each of which causes students to value or devalue learning itself.

When Ivan Illich, in *Deschooling Society*, said, "Learning is the human activity which least needs manipulation by others," he could easily have had in mind that student who learns everything offered or implied as it passes precisely because institutionalized voices were silenced. The only inner voice for such students is personal authority. This is not typical institutionalized behavior, yet somehow such students are free of those voices which plague others for whom learning is not a difficult but an impersonal accomplishment in pursuit of long-range goals.

Silence is the study of the weight of words. To live within language is not to live within speech or distraction. In its rawest sense language must always be the concentration which is the truth about oneself. To weigh the language for truth as in to "weigh anchor," is to float free of a safe moorage, steer clear of shallows and rapids and concentrate all one's attention—as any decent helmsman might, to stretch this metaphor one fathom further—on the course, to follow the truest information about the self available and to speak that. Nothing else matters. In this sense all silence might be rehearsals for speech; one is continuously waiting to have a say in print, for instance, or in some fictional public reading, to speak words weighed so often they could not have been chosen otherwise. Knowledge of the import of one's words, of their full affect on others, the relationship to that concentration we know as "the self," arises for the student out of an inner silence. Without it how can anyone make a valid selection? How can students hope to speak what truth they know? How can they know the meaning of the "self," as Denise Levertov for one example uses it in a line like, "a stone before the carver, you entered into yourself." It seems hard not to believe that the noticeable differences in the quality of silence for students who make it useful to their lives and those burdened by depression, who can do no more than attend, and that infrequently, should be traced back to parents. In conversations with students there is a silence which goes unexpressed after the words "my real Dad." It's a deadening silence, and one in which there is an assumption we can just glide past the distinction between real parents and step-parents. But like a bump in the road no one can avoid, it is difficult to ignore the way each kid treats so acceptable a social arrangement and not note it as a personal tragedy, for which a moment's pause seems not completely out of place. The inability to make public such emptiness, composed of emotional chasms, seems derived from an American inexpressiveness, traditionally attributed to the stereotypical male. In 1934 John Wayne uttered the words, "Never explain, never apologize. It makes you look weak," words written for him in *She Wore a Yellow Ribbon*. When I have written these words on the board, student journal entries have capitalized on its male insensitivity, its denial of the need to express emotion for which many take John Wayne as the clichéd symbol, though some have never heard of him. Most responded that the opposite was true: not apologizing or explaining makes you weak. It's gratifying to see students, both males and females, recognize the contradiction in a teaching passed down through several generations of rugged individuals. Yet an observer can't help but recognize the unapproachable silence surrounding the post-modern role of interchangeable parents, which, for many students, teaches hatred for the birth parent.

In response to another writing prompt, one student wrote, "Silence can be very bad, cutting you off from everyone else, making you conform to something you are not. Two quotes that are on the board in front of me, both contradict and agree with the two sides of silence:

'You have not converted a man, because you have silenced him.'

'Silence is the cornerstone of character.'"

The second of these quotations exemplifies that duality which nothing in our class discussions seems to escape. The philosophy class will soon confront Descartes' *Metaphysical Treatise of the One and the Many*. Is there unity in all things? Or are there, as Descartes says, finite spirits and infinite spirit? Duality seems to light up the material plane. Both the finite and the infinite possess the material world. This type of question burdens a high school philosophy class. I cannot—meaning it is both antithetical to my nature and seems out of the question to do otherwise—stop talking or apply my aggravated notions of silence to this class. Continually speaking in front of them, I ask questions for which I try not to provide answers, breaking silence into fragments of rhetoric and empty space. I'm always questioning, but am I getting students to question and draw conclusions? Sometimes I feel certain they are doing that, yet frequently my own classroom talk gets in the way of knowing real things. "Words," John Gardner tells us, "seem inevitably to distance us from the brute existent (real trees, stones, yawing babies) that words symbolize and in our thought processes tend to replace. At any rate, so philosophers like Hobbes, Nietzsche, and Heidegger have maintained, (and our experiences with punsters seem to confirm the opinion)." The difference between experiences in which language can distance us from real things and those which bring the real world closer may depend on a concentration by someone cognizant of how words concretize symbols.

While listening to two profound language experiences—a radio report on the Branch Davidian trial and my son, Teddy, three and a half, concentrating on making his Valentine—I had an eerie sense of the disparities of language that can be at once familiar and alien. The news carried quotes from those Davidians in the Waco house gathering their fuel supply to, as the reporter suggested, "immolate" themselves. I was impressed by how their speech seemed familiar. It was unhurried, casual and committed, and hauntingly positivist in the same way the generation of the sixties and seventies adapted usage to collective concerns with uncompromising resistance while retaining the accent of Standard English. While the radio gave me this story, my son leaned against the edge of the oak table and continued a project he and his mother had begun yesterday, sticking flimsy hearts to a huge red cupid. Totally absorbed, he didn't speak a word for thirty minutes, very unusual for him. At the end he called it his I Love You Card and gave me two of these immense productions. His manipulation of symbols within a great space, within a silence so productive that "I love you" could be the only result, created an enviable concentration of all his important symbols. How related I felt both to him and these people who frightened me by their similarities to Jonestown. I recalled the comedy I'd seen that weekend, where Jim Jones was mentioned in a passing joke. The parlance of media consciousness gives us ourselves saying things in a besieged compound we might never dream otherwise and in our own familial voices: "Is there enough kerosene?" So much like myself in earlier years, filling lamps to read Dante far into the night.

Endless talk in philosophy class or poetry where today I wound up mistakenly referring to Williams as Whitman repeatedly for ten minutes, despite the kids' correcting me, can easily disperse our fragile attempts to concentrate. So I write as often as I can while students do, neglecting their papers which pile up uncorrected, ungraded. I ask if they believe I *can* correct their papers. Today in philosophy kids were talking to one another in small groups and less inflicted with my voice. I went around and babbled ideas and half-ass explanations at each group. This is called cooperative learning, and when the groups change to say different things to other students, the teacher is said to jigsaw the class. One of the main triumphs is less "teacher talk." We're told teachers want methods other than the lecture style to avoid their own chatter, but do any lead to that silence which my son demonstrated? Isn't concentration the real act of correcting?

John Gardner tells us fiction that lasts tends to be "moral," that is it "works with a minimum of cynical manipulation and it tends to reach affirmations favorable rather than opposed to life." Whether these criteria would enable a reading of Nietzsche or Kafka is perhaps better avoided for now. Concern with student ideas makes me wonder if I can teach affirmation. Isn't the side of any writer that affirms the one which was nurtured at some time well before teachers who are busy enough inculcating rules of grammar, style, and logic? To teach affirmation becomes its opposite: to restrict negative imagery, to censor racism, bigotry, to patrol for Satanism, suicide, sexual deviance, drug use, bullying, serious violence, even mass murder. We sometimes turn the argument regarding a student's predisposition to affirm or not back to parents who pass on a gift for affirmation or the habit of belittling, disparaging, and finding fault. What parents willingly or subconsciously hand down, they must certainly assume responsibility over. Yet if school is considered the primary locus of opportunity, educators assume the teaching of values. Almost in contradiction to such a goal, schools promote a continuously distractive atmosphere, dependent on sudden entrances and exits, announcements in harsh voices over the intercom, surprise notes or phone calls to the class, teacher, or individual students from any of an array of authorities in the attendance office, counseling office, disciplinary office, library, special education, athletic department, or custodial service. In the midst of an atmosphere comparable to the chaos of a shopping mall, students devoted to learning progress by observing in the scholarship of their teachers the worth of silence. Teachers who demand a scholarly atmosphere in their classrooms are also the models for what discipline really means. They present themselves—in the midst of an environment which devalues silence so much that a quiet room may mean "nothing's happening," that "study" is not a verb, that not love of knowledge but knowledge of long-range goals governs education. It seems likely that if some dominant aspect of the human spirit can survive adolescence, it will rise above chaos, and affirm.

*

Another world unfolds through thrilled and empty space. We could almost say by naming a place we crowd out silence; every wild river, valley, or chain of granite and basalt named in the European tongue of its claimant echoes through primeval silence the contractor's hammer and faller's chainsaw. I don't know if it's so different to use descriptions for names, as the pre-authoritarian traditions have; it certainly seems quieter, and less in need of a standing army, since the silence needed to witness a place is similar to prayer. You could think wilderness was a kind of church except the way anthropocentrism has turned old-growth trees into cash crops and low-cost housing. To reinvest one's gift for worship by isolating one place from another separates wilderness from our own nature, as if we're not in the same world but bear our burden, as private citizens are led to believe, in solitude provided by cities, towns, and deteriorated communities.

Years ago I read a description by the wilderness writer Barry Lopez of stopping to remove from the highway every road-kill he came upon. I was disturbed by this because talking about an act which has personal significance makes it merely anecdotal; aside from the impossibility of performing such a deed for the hundreds of dead animals most of us pass on North American highways, how could he ever get anywhere on time? I winced not only because the act seemed too private to be instructive, as if readers must be told how to live, but because I have often grappled with my own frustration at being helpless in the face of the mass accidental slaughter of animals on highways which have devoured one kind of silence to create another. Ignoring all peripheral details is of course vital to driver and passengers, yet the restraint it takes to ignore is continuously and profoundly critiqued by these sentinels rotting in the breakdown lanes. I have often wondered where societies should draw the line. When should traffic halt? That is, when will it become incumbent upon us to notice the sheer numbers of road dead? Would a human body always stop traffic? Would our schedules and weariness as travelers become less important if those animals we find were not trivialized, if the smear of blood, feather, or fur weren't allowed to blend into the paving? It's his attention to these victims I admire in Lopez, and I can't help but imagine him, as impossible as it seems to do, pulling over for the large body of a dog or deer, the small shape of raccoon, or the less beautiful, even deranged human face of 'possum, putting on gloves he keeps in his vehicle only for this, and lifting each animal quietly and humbly off the road, away from the breakdown lane to the more suitable resting place in well-trimmed lawns, overgrown weeds, cattails, or even under boughs of cedar, redwood, and fir.

I can see that this is a kind of reparation, a term derived from a tradition of reading the world religiously, and I view it as a personal confrontation, not with the destruction of that silence which has allowed the highway to wedge itself between one source of food and another, but with the face of death, with the remains of each of these beasts who have no souls, as the Catholic church taught fellows like Lopez and me. This convenient form of discrimination has assisted the mass slaughter of wildlife as well as domestic animals for at least this recently completed millennium. The grander ideal persists that the world as it is, the silence of a wilderness, is far closer to our human understanding of what a cathedral is than our more commonly frequented places of worship.

Perhaps my disturbance arose from my not having found an equally responsible method of dealing with powerlessness in the face of so many deaths. Recently I listened to a radio commentator's interview with Barry Lopez in which he recounted the road-kill experiences I had read. I was surprised my reaction hadn't changed. Listening to Lopez, whose writing has sustained me in difficult times, I became incensed, and began composing in my mind a letter about what I saw as the imposition on society of individual behaviors that should best be done in silence. When I got to the part of my tirade where I accused him of acting like a modern Francis of Assisi, I was driving too fast on a back country road, and a sparrow smashed into my windshield, slid along the glass, and lodged itself in the hinge of the rear view mirror on the passenger side. A streak of blood across my vision, I had to wait a half mile before reaching a safe place to stop. Someone was there with his hunting dog, about to take a walk down a logging road, and I parked far enough away that I wouldn't have to explain I was cleaning the carcass of a little bird from the front of my truck; now I am cupping my hands together, cradling its smooth feathers, long beak near the wide open eye, to a place of tall grasses and weed.

After that I began driving with a pair of gloves in my truck. Although I have not yet made a habit, as Lopez and others have, of removing bodies of animals carefully from the road, I have become a kind of convert. But it is like the conversion of the formerly self-conscious nonbeliever; perhaps I would be embarrassed to be found practicing the faith or to be thought naive should my students drive by as I lift the body of someone's pet away from further damage. Maybe I'll get over it. Maybe I'll discover it would be good for my students to know me this way. Maybe the humility one might achieve from being so recognized would benefit us all. For them the world blunders along on its superhighway and back roads heedless of what gets in the way. They must too, or so they say when asked why not stop for every dead animal on the road. Silence enters the classroom when we discuss those small acts we can do to repair what the world flying by has damaged, a silence helpless and complicitous. School may not approach this silence without recognizing its own involvement, without noting that to condone destructive western progress is a grave sin of omission, because it teaches a way to ignore. Apart from transmitting fundamental knowledge about the world, we encourage innocence, yet ironically promote the ignorance which maintains the status quo.

Within the silence found in his poem, "Traveling in The Dark," the late William Stafford recounts an occasion to take responsibility for one of those beside the road. This silence is filled with the rush of the highway and the hesitation of the poet to act, perhaps when no one else was, or when maybe one more life, unborn, had also to be taken. At the end of the poem, he calls that moment his "only swerving," when he has paused to think "for us all." It's an interesting term, also used in the first stanza to state the obvious: removing the dead deer would prevent another driver swerving off the road. But in the final couplet, Stafford swerves, at least momentarily, away from his responsibility to other drivers; "us all" is a larger crowd by now. "Around our group," he says just before the final act, a group whose members he has already delineated: the killed doe, himself, her fawn, and his somewhat self-empowered, all but anthropomorphic car. Although the doe has "stiffened already," the fawn "lay there waiting, / alive, still, never to be born," while the car "lowers" its headlights, "purrs," and "glares" like the conscience of the Industrial Era: man must be loyal to man above all, and to take time pondering what effect our travels at night on mountain roads have on the innocent "might make more dead," and slow the progress we are steadily making in the dark.

"Around our group I could hear the wilderness listen." This line imagines silence alive. The wilderness listens: expectancy, emptiness, again the personification of, in this case, the entire universe, uncharacteristically attentive to these few lives. Stafford can only achieve his purpose by turning silence into just such an awareness of human intervention in its own interest. To imagine silence otherwise is to exclude wilderness from "us all" in the next line. To view himself as not being able to "hear the wilderness listen," is to isolate himself from whatever the world does and to which we apply our metaphors in order feebly to capture the limitation by which we understand how the mind disconnects.

Sacred places or special places like the edge of Wilson River road in "Traveling through the Dark" can take on the awe and impart the silence which we used to associate with churches. A silence deserving more respect among many of my students than that of school or library. The silence embodied in education is somewhat like that of the highway. We are forced to ignore peripheral "non-factors" and concentrate on the road ahead, or more poetically, the "main stream." As I write about the silence within wilderness and begin to understand the kinds of religious reparation many people are already trying to make, and as I begin to see how much the silence which is firmly a part of a world outside human life can repeatedly be brought back or reconnected as is the root meaning, *religare*, to education and our efforts to prepare people who will be more than just commuters entering the flow of traffic, yet another gunman opens fire in a mosque, a school library, or cafeteria, killing and maiming hundreds, and once again for religious or other sanctimonious convictions the silence is shattered.

A metaphor connects religion and education as it does nature and human nature: reparation. Perhaps this metaphor is to be found within the agenda of America's public schools; we must after all repair damages at a variety of levels while remediating assumptions about basic skills. I have trouble understanding the metaphor sometimes as I believe my students do when I begin, usually without warning, to rhapsodize, clicking off one connection after another, attempting to reinforce the possibility that metaphors are all the mind ever makes, or so Robert Frost has said. The highway, the road kill, the driver prayerfully returning it to earth, the wilderness which has been opened (in the surgical sense) for the sake of our timely arrivals, all useful concepts for education.

For me the highway is that quick road to anywhere education keeps trying to reach. Every note from the "front office" has the newly adopted motto, "Education is a journey, not a destination." The statement continues to baffle me. Perhaps the journey is the highway. In which case, the process of their education cuts through the wild parts of children's lives and makes it difficult to move from one feeding ground to the next and those who do not make it die by the side of the road. This reading seems applicable, but a cliché. After all, the students themselves are shuttling along on this freeway and whatever it is that's trying to sneak across to the other side is going to run into them at high speed when they eat up the road. "How quickly they grow." By high school how firmly entrenched are habits of self-doubt and delusion, the vehicle, as Buddhists say. It glides down the avenue of schoolwork in the total silence that white noise is, a droning heater at the back of the room, the computer beeping, announcements over the intercom, the teacher's monotone, the headphone nuisance scraping static into the auditory canal, the constant self-talk of failure or firm and absolute assurance.

But what is the road kill? What sacrifices its life by running in front of their minds? The teacher's soul. The love of an idea, the glory of language, the validity of our animal natures, the faith in pure act, the nurture of the spirit by music, science, theater, dance, mathematics, art, love, true and deep feeling, the ultimate value of real and concentrated silence. It is finally the teacher who pulls over from time to time and with modesty removes the body of silence and teaches that raccoons, 'possum, deer, and other cherished emblems of the uncomplaining wilderness are avoidable. Not all of them, only that one or two who truly can't stop looking at the real world will be momentarily struck by the absurdity of propelling along in the vehicle called Education, or struck by the teacher's effort to live within that silence he or she can only reach by shaping a mind like that of animals who attempt to cross obstacles in search of a disappearing world.

I have lost the hearing in my left ear. There is a continuous ringing, and because I have abandoned what creative urges "drive" my life, it is boring. My spiritual side casts its inner-looking eyeball about in the dark for its own tail. It is all so different than I once expected—my life. I expected a continual moving forward, not this endlessly the same. Is this what my students experience? Headphones like earplugs? Imaginations on overdrive or driven to catatonia? Does shutting out noise create enough humdrum to cope? Trapped in a dark place like Plato's cave, they experience a pale shadow of the well-lit world. Some students live with a keen anticipation. Either at the end of the school day, or more gloriously after graduation, it will reach fulfillment as "freedom," the vast uncharted, beyond the diploma. Yet "security" (maybe a more crucial word for other students) may well be found in the schedule, the building, desks, and the habit of school. I know this is true to a degree by ways my students greet me not long after beginning my courses. It could never be truer that as far as they are concerned, I am a complete stranger. They know nothing about me: my ideas, my preferences, my past, my feelings about them are unknowns and givens teachers and students accept at the start of a new course. They know no real facts about me, even when I tell them, because most hardly remember such things. Personal details or history of an adult is extraneous to the grade, and of no social interest to someone whose ocean of consciousness is fed from the rapid of peer satisfaction, pressure, and denial. Why then do so many assume familiar attitudes when we first meet? Although many students seem to do this to some extent, the familiarity, and perhaps a particular brand of trust, is more obvious in the youngest, the freshmen.

213

I am also continuously overwhelmed at how by next semester or next year, last year's freshmen don't nod or say hello when passing in the hall. Those silences when I pass someone who was my student and doesn't acknowledge our previous acquaintance have become so common that I no longer feel hurt or offended. An unacknowledged interdependence in all honesty becomes burdensome beyond the time when student and teacher are in contact. The teacher cannot, without the student, exemplify an idea, clarify a thought, or in some cases speak independently of his or her relationship to students, much as an idea can have no physical existence apart from the mind, the way some 18th century philosophers saw it. Even younger students recognize the temporality of the teacher-student relationship, yet confusion about what to say when passing in the hall renders up only this blind scurrying past one another like cats in big cities or people in malls. Students are organisms attempting to survive in a crowded tank. Sometimes the organism is forced to emulate the machinery of its captivity. We slide along the marble floors like ball bearings precisioned in their grooves and come to rest before the programmed "spin" cycle, at our desks, or "work stations" as classrooms are now euphemistically industrialized to. When the tub is agitated those components we wished cleaned will tumble to our will. The teacher's experience of the agitation and the moment at rest before a new cycle begins should be appreciated as controlled by outside forces.

Needless to say, making metaphor about education works in all directions, benefits all biases. For it is impossible to speak about education without reflecting bias. When the words used to describe a school are derived from vocabulary which evokes machinery, the biases reflected have to be classified as anti-humanist. Hundreds of abstractions, acronyms, and abbreviations comprise a jargon with which only educators are fluent; much like the legal or medical professions, this shorthand—which one insightful pedagogue labeled "educado"—stands as a formidable deterrent to public or parental involvement in the periodic restructuring (more machined metaphors arise) public education is prone to conduct.

Only yesterday I was in attendance at a conference with a parent and her son. She brought along her little daughter. The tone of seriousness was perhaps assured by the counselor, devoid of humor, who hadn't realized that the mother would need a Spanish translator. When it was suggested her son could translate, the woman said in English he might lie. While we waited for one of the bilingual school secretaries to show up, the three teachers and one student teacher could say little to the student or indeed to his mom. His sister was never acknowledged. The secretary did an excellent job translating our remarks to the young woman; the questions from the counselor in English were in that psychobabble which only the converted can sincerely appreciate. Instead of his stating what he might do to improve, the student estimated he needed "mas attencion," and this only to the secretary and his mother. To the counselor he presented a face of contrite doubt; as a reward for which she adjourned the meeting. While they spoke in Spanish, the counselor and we three teachers, locked out, could say nothing. Since none of us was attending to the Spanish, we were left during the several minutes they hashed things out to our own thoughts, to stare into our grade books, plan our lessons. We'd come to this meeting to report on the student's grades and help fashion a method to overcome his difficulties. Left out at least temporarily by virtue of their language, a difference more private than any of us had expected, we were essentially distant observers of the educational process. Just as parents who attend our public meetings are often sidelined by jargon, the ruthless nomenclature and argot many teachers and administrators trill with mastery.

It didn't occur to us and will be impossible to prove that we'd come to that meeting to discuss in deadly earnest the metaphorical qualities of the first six letters of the alphabet. The school-wide image of a B student may not have been what we saw before us: a freshman born in a Central American town to Spanish-speaking parents who fled for their lives when he was four, a boy whose English was very good and lately has been expressing interest in gang membership, who dresses, acts, and talks like a gangster, and who, as the secretary translated for me when it was my turn to speak about his recently failing English performance, never turns in assignments which he appears to be doing in a notebook he will not show me. My Spanish is very weak, but I could understand her pointing out that the boy had received a "B" in English from me last semester and so has the ability. The metaphor of a grade is indeed distinct from its symbolic value, which may be more like a universal concept. We all knew what corresponded to each of the letters used at our school for grading purposes. It is the pluses and minuses which cause hair-splitting and are controlled by the variables of temperament. But to consider the power of the metaphor, it is necessary to overlap two disparate concepts. One is the universal B student—not an overachiever, but unsatisfied with the mediocrity a C symbolizes—and the other is the apparent gangster we saw before us. I think the other teachers saw him as a C student at best. In some classes the grade was determined by accruing points when assignments met deadlines; this student met none.

Like grades, the word "deadline" is a universal. It comes into schools through industry whose protégé public education often slavishly is. For most teachers late assignments are refused. At another parent conference I met a teacher who asked about my attitude toward deadlines. "I don't enable that," she said, meaning me and my laissez-faire methods no disrespect I'm sure, but nevertheless cuffing me with her co-dependent lingo. She didn't question me further, but I feel quite certain that she would willingly tell me that we are preparing them for the real world where deadlines are sacramental. I can have no argument with that. Unless, of course, I were to spoof the real world and all of its works to suggest we are teaching those who now occupy and will not fail to own seats in the virtual reality of a new century's popular culture, where morality is as adjustable as the dial, the work ethic as perishable as fame.

The student in question, David, glanced occasionally at me across the long boardroom table where his other teachers, his mom, and counselor sat. I was afraid, or perhaps he was, that he might want me to tell how he came to have that B in English last semester. Uncomfortable in coming to this meeting, I was certain everything I said would be colored, at least for him, by the experience we had together about which I refused to say a word. Would he remember I told him this semester he would have to work for a B or a passing grade and I would help him? Or would he only remember we played a basketball game and blurt out in front of everybody, mother and all, and I'd lose my job, that last semester, only when I was certain David was going to squeak by with a D according to the numbers, I had asked him if he'd like to play some basketball with me, one on one. "Oh, maybe . . . sure," he said humoring the teacher. "Would you like to play for your grade?" I had his attention now; he looked up at me this time, quizzical. "You win, you get a D; I win, you get an F." "You won't win," he said immediately—he was hooked.

I made it through that meeting without being exposed as a teacher who grades without principles. After the bait had been set I'd suggested that David could get a C, if he wrote about our game and a B if his writing was good. His recorded grade reflects that final piece of writing which was witty, exaggerated, and as grammatically indifferent as most student work, but most importantly, a compelling story. When we were driving away from the basketball court, he told me he'd never played basketball with a teacher before. Something might last; even in prison a gang boy would remember he got that B. Grades, I was told in "teacher school," are arbitrary, subjective, and irrelevant. If grading is the ultimate function of the teacher, and he or she is an accountant, nothing of the variety of songs and

217

dances with which teachers attempt to influence, to actually affect the direction of someone's life, to channel desire, matters. Every morning I think only about what I'm doing that day in certain classes. For others, I wait until minutes before the bell. Sometimes I begin a class without knowing what's coming next. These are confessions, my training tells me, I shouldn't be proud of. Even someone who avoids developing those kinds of lesson plans I learned while studying for the teaching certificate makes some effort at organizing the material to be taught well in advance of the day. It will seem like specious rationalization to suggest that I believe in the importance of presenting my high school students the image of an educated person speaking on many topics without notes and in such a way that the students can approach the topic closely enough to have an idea. Should I instead assume they must have an opinion, state it, develop concise theses and topic sentences and discover evidence to support each opinion? Yes, many students must be directed toward such goals. Like arrows guided incrementally toward a target the absurdist Zeno says they never reach, each grade is a fraction of the journey. Nothing is more on target or such a direct hit as when a student recognizes that opinion statements which do not afford opposing views the possibility of accuracy, are lopsided, vain, hollow registers of learned ignorance.

Many are the "ideal" students in terms of behavior, just as they are the ones who have always done their homework. Many are girls who, having been taken for granted for so long, have never been pushed beyond their limits. Faced with a teacher who will not set goals or deadlines, hardworking students write that teacher off as too easy, "unpredictable," or "eccentric," and therefore dangerous to the GPA, which is predicated on completing each assignment and meeting every deadline as if one's life depended on entrusting the future to the calm predictability of public education. To stand before them and just talk seems to require nothing, and seems less important to a GPA- driven student; it will not be on the test.

Perhaps my greatest frustration as a teacher is not that David will probably fail despite parent-teacher conferences and a burst of enthusiasm and resolve, but that for the vast majority the grade is everything. I don't know what it is in my background, and this may cause me to sound far more precious than I'd like to, but for reasons unclear to me, I rarely attempt to discuss grades with students unless they are failing. It's like the way I am loathe to ask the cost of something which does not have a price tag clearly marked. During those times in my life when I have done free-lance work of one kind or another, it was always very difficult to assign a price. I didn't like to haggle over the money, nor do I like to haggle over grades. The work is really what is important, not my metaphorical stamp of approval. And yet it is that stamp which students believe matters more than knowledge. Perhaps it is wisest to inculcate at an early age the value of metaphor and its omnipresence. *Cheater*, a movie about the real and symbolic values of test scores, indicates that students have confused the meanings of "democracy" with "meritocracy." What if students could see that the grade today may indeed translate into something of value in the industrialized world, that employers like to know the record, but that tomorrow all that could change and the values of grades, already suspiciously inflated, could be replaced by demonstrations of knowledge?

What is knowledge? Sometimes I intentionally confuse my classes telling them the only knowledge is self-knowledge; Thales' "Know thyself" has more to do with education than their Byzantine transcripts in the registrar's computer. My son gives me the most apt examples for the primacy of learning and the power of self-knowledge. Just before he falls asleep, his head turned on the pillow away from me lying in the dark beside him, he rises up and turns toward me. "Daddy," he whispers in the silence where I thought he'd already fallen asleep. "These are my doors," his fingers sliding across from eye to eye, two half-closed slits of deep blue. Besides my frequent shock at how cute he can be just before sleep, I am additionally overwhelmed by what he does not say. By the process which must have led to anintuitionsharedso universally as to echo William Blake, Aldous Huxley, and Jim Morrison. "These are my doors, Daddy," and the smile before he drops off to sleep, once more telling me how much (showing on his fingers) he loves his mother and me. What could he have been thinking before saying that? He'd been silent for so long, lying in the dark. What images, what pictures were unraveling through him before achieving that recognition which metaphor must always be? The recognition of a likeness which goes well beyond that of similarity. If similarity were all there were to metaphor, why would we conceive of a distinct figure of speech? The simile is by its nature only useful, it is a tool; even to talk about simile I must make metaphor, but not as a comparison. Metaphor is our habit of definition. We do not simply throw up one item against the backdrop of another, overlaying two disparate conceptions, but we define one thing or concept or even another's being by the limits of some other. It is more than useful, more than a tool handy to assist understanding or explication. It is understanding, not the process but the moment of recognition. "These are my doors!" What an achievement of mind it is, even though he will have forgotten his own words by morning, to define perception and the world as that which passes through.

If metaphor is how we think, as Frost said, then aren't we continually defining by means of things other than those to be defined, linking until similes and logic give way to chaos which metaphor compels us to recognize? What wilderness the mind recognizes itself to be swimming within can hardly be turned back and referred to any longer as a system, or like systems. "If the doors of perception were cleansed, everything would appear . . . as it truly is, infinite," says Blake. The metaphor can be found behind the eye, and is the eye itself; like the barn door or the entrance to the tavern, the yawning mouth of hell or the stairway to heaven, the senses swing both ways.

Michael Daley was born in Boston and is the author of one collection of poetry, *The Straits.* He published several chapbooks between 1985 and 2004: *Yes: Five Poems*, *Angels, Amigos, Original Sin, The Corn Maiden*, *Horace: Eleven Odes* (translations) and *Rosehip Plum Cherry.* His poems have appeared in *American Poetry Review, The Hudson Review, Ploughshares, Manoa, Alaskan Quarterly, Nebraska Review*, *Prairie Schooner, Poetry East, Raven Chronicles, Seattle Review*, and on Garrison Keilor's *The Writer's Almanac.* He holds degrees from the University of Massachusetts and the University of Washington, and has received awards from Bumbershoot, Fessenden, the Seattle Arts Commission, the National Endowment of Humanities, and the Fulbright Program.

AEQUITAS BOOKS is a new imprint of Pleasure Boat Studio which focuses on nonfiction books with philosophical or sociological themes. *Way Out There* is the second book published under this imprint. Following is a complete list of books by Pleasure Boat Studio: A Literary Press:

The Case of Emily V. * Keith Oatley
*ISBN 9781-929355-30-3 * 378 pages * mystery * $18 * a caravel mystery*
Against Romance * Michael Blumenthal
*ISBN 1-929355-23-8 * 110 pages * poetry * $14*
Speak to the Mountain: The Tommie Waites Story * Dr. Bessie Blake
*ISBN 1-929355-29-7 / 36-X * 278 pages*
** biography * $18 / $26 * AN AEQUITAS BOOK*
Artrage * Everett Aison
*ISBN 1-929355-25-4 * 225 pages * fiction * $15*
Days We Would Rather Know * Michael Blumenthal
*ISBN 1-929355-24-6 * 118 pages * poetry * $14*
Puget Sound: 15 Stories * C. C. Long
*ISBN 1-929355-22-X * 150 pages * fiction * $14*
Homicide My Own * Anne Argula
*ISBN 1-929355-21-1 * 220 pages * fiction (mystery) * $16*
Craving Water * Mary Lou Sanelli
*ISBN 1-929355-19-X * 121 pages * poetry * $15*
When the Tiger Weeps * Mike O'Connor
*ISBN 1-929355-18-9 * 168 pages * poetry and prose * 15*
Wagner, Descending: The Wrath of the Salmon Queen * Irving Warner
*ISBN 1-929355-17-3 * 242 pages * fiction * $16*
Concentricity * Sheila E. Murphy
*ISBN 1-929355-16-5 * 82 pages * poetry * $13.95*
Schilling, from a study in lost time * Terrell Guillory
*ISBN 1-929355-09-2 * 156 pages * fiction * $16.95*
Rumours: A Memoir of a British POW in WWII * Chas Mayhead
*ISBN 1-929355-06-8 * 201 pages * nonfiction * $16*
The Immigrant's Table * Mary Lou Sanelli
*ISBN 1-929355-15-7 * $13.95 * poetry and recipes * $13/95*
The Enduring Vision of Norman Mailer * Dr. Barry H. Leeds
*ISBN 1-929355-11-4 * criticism * $18*
Women in the Garden * Mary Lou Sanelli
*ISBN 1-929355-14-9 * poetry * $13.95*

Pronoun Music * Richard Cohe
ISBN 1-929355-03-3 * short stories * $16
If You Were With Me Everything Would Be All Right * Ken Harvey
ISBN 1-929355-02-5 * short stories * $16
The 8th Day of the Week * Al Kessler
ISBN 1-929355-00-9 * fiction * $16
Another Life, and Other Stories * Edwin Weihe
ISBN 1-929355-011-7 * short stories * $16
Saying the Necessary * Edward Harkness
ISBN 0-9651413-7-3 (hard) $22; 0-9651413-9-X (paper) * poetry * $14
Nature Lovers * Charles Potts
ISBN 1-929355-04-1 * poetry * $10
In Memory of Hawks, & Other Stories from Alaska * Irving Warner
ISBN 0-9651413-4-9 * 210 pages * fiction * $15
The Politics of My Heart *William Slaughter
ISBN 0-9651413-0-6 * 96 pages * poetry * $12.95
The Rape Poems * Frances Driscoll
ISBN 0-9651413-1-4 * 88 pages * poetry * $12.95
When History Enters the House: Essays from
Central Europe * Michael Blumenthal
ISBN 0-9651413-2-2 * 248 pages * nonfiction * $15
Setting Out: The Education of Li-li * Tung
Nien * Trans fm Chinese by Mike O'Connor
ISBN 0-9651413-3-0 * 160 pages * fiction * $15

Our Chapbook Series:
No. 1: The Handful of Seeds: Three and a Half Essays * Andrew Schelling
ISBN 0-9651413-5-7 * $7 * 36 pages * nonfiction
No. 2: Original Sin * Michael Daley
ISBN 0-9651413-6-5 * $8 * 36 pages * poetry
No. 3: Too Small to Hold You * Kate Reavey
ISBN 1-92935-05-x * $8 * poetry
No. 4: The Light on Our Faces: A Therapy Dialogue * Lee Miriam Whitman-
Raymond
ISBN 1-929355-12-2 * $8 * 36 pages * poetry
No. 5: Selected New Poems of Rainer Maria Rilke * Trans fm
German by Alice Derry
ISBN 1-929355-10-6 * $10 * poetry

No. 6: *Through High Still Air: A Season at Sourdough Mountain* * Tim McNulty ISBN 1-929355-27-0 * $9 * poetry and prose
No. 7: *Sight Progress* * Zhang Er, Trans fm Chinese by Rachel Levitsky ISBN 1-929355-28-9 * $9 * prose-poems
No. 8: *The Perfect Hour* * Blas Falconer ISBN 1-929355-31-9 * $9 * poetry

FROM OUR BACKLIST (IN LIMITED EDITIONS):

Desire * Jody Aliesan
ISBN 0-912887-11-7 * $14 * poetry (an Empty Bowl book)
Deams of the Hand * Susan Goldwitz
ISBN 0-912887-12-5 * $14 * poetry (an Empty Bowl book)
Lineage * Mary Lou Sanelli
No ISBN * $14 * poetry (an Empty Bowl book)
The Basin: Poems from a Chinese Province * Mike O'Connor
ISBN 0-912887 - 20-6 * $10 / $20 * poetry (paper / hardbound) (an Empty Bowl book)
The Straits * Michael Daley
ISBN 0-912887-04-4 * $10 * poetry (an Empty Bowl book)
In Our Hearts and Minds: The Northwest and Central America * Ed. Michael Daley
ISBN 0-912887-18-4 * $12 * poetry and prose (an Empty Bowl book)
The Rainshadow * Mike O'Connor
No ISBN * $16 * poetry (an Empty Bowl book)
Untold Stories *William Slaughter
ISBN 1-912887 24-9 * $10 * poetry (an Empty Bowl book)
In Blue Mountain Dusk * Tim McNulty
ISBN 0-9651413-8-1 * $12.95 * poetry (a Broken Moon book)

Orders: Pleasure Boat Studio books are available by order from your bookstore, directly from PBS (at the email below), or through the following:
SPD (Small Press Distribution) Tel. 800-869-7553, Fax 510-524-0852
Partners / West Tel. 425-227-8486, Fax 425-204-2448
Baker & Taylor 800-775-1100, Fax 800-775-7480
Ingram Tel 615-793-5000, Fax 615-287-5429
amazon.com or barnesandnoble.com
PLEASURE BOAT STUDIO: A LITERARY PRESS
201 West 89th Street
New York, NY 10024
Tel: 212-362-8563 / Fax: 888-810-5308
www.pleasureboatstudio.com / pleasboat@nyc.rr.com

Typeset in *Perpetua* at Old Dog New Trick, the first Tiger Lillies still in bloom, MMVI.